Worn Out

Labor and Technology

Winifred Poster, Series Editor

Madison Van Oort, *Worn Out: How Retailers Surveil and Exploit Workers in the Digital Age and How Workers Are Fighting Back*

Worn Out

How Retailers Surveil and Exploit Workers in the Digital Age and How Workers Are Fighting Back

Madison Van Oort

The MIT Press

Cambridge, Massachusetts | London, England

The MIT Press would like to thank the anonymous peer reviewers who provided comments on drafts of this book. The generous work of academic experts is essential for establishing the authority and quality of our publications. We acknowledge with gratitude the contributions of these otherwise uncredited readers.

This book was set in ITC Stone Serif Std and ITC Stone Sans Std by New Best-set Typesetters Ltd. Printed and bound in the United States of America.

Library of Congress Cataloging-in-Publication Data

Names: Van Oort, Madison, author.
Title: Worn out : how retailers surveil and exploit workers in the digital age and how workers are fighting back / Madison Van Oort.
Description: Cambridge, Massachusetts : The MIT Press, [2023] | Series: Labor and technology | Includes bibliographical references and index | Summary: "Worn Out connects scholarship on digital capitalism and surveillance to the specific setting of retail work in fast fashion"— Provided by publisher.
Identifiers: LCCN 2022028464 (print) | LCCN 2022028465 (ebook) | ISBN 9780262544931 (paperback) | ISBN 9780262372763 (epub) | ISBN 9780262372770 (pdf)
Subjects: LCSH: Retail trade—United States—Employees. | Electronic surveillance—United States. | Retail trade—Social aspects—United States. | Retail trade—United States—Management.
Classification: LCC HD8039.M4 .U583 2023 (print) | LCC HD8039.M4 (ebook) | DDC 381/.10973—dc23/eng/20221021
LC record available at https://lccn.loc.gov/2022028464
LC ebook record available at https://lccn.loc.gov/2022028465

10 9 8 7 6 5 4 3 2 1

Contents

Acknowledgments

I owe this book first and foremost to everyone I encountered in my fieldwork. Thank you to my coworkers, interviewees, the Retail Action Project, and the people of New York City and Minneapolis. I will donate all proceeds of this book to people and organizations fighting for better futures. Have a suggestion? Find me on LinkedIn and let me know.

Thank you to my PhD advisors, Teresa Gowan and David Naguib Pellow. I'm especially grateful for Teresa's constant encouragement to "be bold, be wrong" and David's modeling of how to conduct research in critical solidarity with social movements. Thank you to my committee members Lisa Sun-Hee Park, Tracey Deutsch, and Claudia Neuhauser. Thank you also to Ruha Benjamin, Karla Erickson, Susan Ferguson, Winifred Poster, Kesho Scott, and Rachel Shurman. When I think about the kind of scholar and mentor I want to be, I think of you all.

Thank you to everyone who read and gave feedback on earlier versions of this book and/or helped me think through ideas, including Tanja Andic, Jeff Berryhill, Kriti Budhiraja, Carolyn Fraker, Jasmine Gibson, Julie Giraldo, Erin Hoekstra, Mingwei Huang, Hanna Hurr, Maggie Kim, Snigdha Kumar, Zhandarka Kurti, Lars Mackenzie, Rahsaan Mahadeo, Alicia Martinson, Andrew Meeker, Devika Narayan, Vicky Osterweil, Conor Tomás Reed, Anuradha Sajjanhar, Shemon Salam, Justine Scattarelli, Emily Springer, and three anonymous reviewers.

Thank you to the University of Minnesota's Institute for Advanced Study, the Minnesota Department of Sociology, the Diversity of Views and Experiences fellowship, the IAS/Informatics Institute "Where Is the Human in the Data?" fellowship, and the Ronald E. Anderson Technology and Social Cohesion fellowship for giving me the support to conduct the research that would eventually turn into this book.

Thank you to my editor, Katie Helke, and everyone else at the MIT Press, for believing in this project and shepherding it, and me, through publication.

Thank you to my family, old roommates, and friends who have cheered me on through this endeavor, including Brandon, Cameryn, Clara, Cutlet, Dane, Daniel, Emily, Gabriella, Jamie, Jordan, Justine, Lindsey, Lisa, Mallory, Parvoneh, Randy, Shonna, Sun, Tim, Todd, and Vern.

I dedicate this book to Jesús Estrada Pérez. We miss you.

Introduction

"I had to work until 4 a.m. last night," the tall, quiet, nineteen-year-old with braces told me with a sigh. "At Forever 21?" I asked. I was shocked. I had worked a handful of entry-level jobs myself, had shopped at places like Forever 21, and had close friends who were labor organizers in other areas of the service sector, like fast food. But I must admit, until I had gotten to know several of my community college students that semester who worked in fast fashion, I hadn't been aware of just how grueling clothing retail work had become.

In fact, my student told me the location where she worked was open until 2 a.m. each day, and she regularly stayed until 4 a.m. processing incoming shipments. On other occasions she mentioned how stressed she was about her work schedule, which changed weekly; she never knew how many hours she'd be assigned nor what her paychecks would be. She lived in Queens with her mother, spending hours on the train each day, rushing from home to school in lower Manhattan and then to work near Times Square and back again; no wonder she was consistently tardy for class.

As Black Friday approached, she told me she feared not only high customer traffic but also "riots" in her store; that fall saw the eruption of Black Lives Matter protests across New York City and around the United States. Those protestors made embodied connections between policing, surveillance, and capitalism by blocking roads, occupying police precincts, and, in many places, disrupting malls and retail stores.

At first glance, fast fashion—a sector of the retail industry known for selling colossal amounts of cheap, trendy clothing—might seem mundane, apolitical, or even a distraction from more pressing social issues. But through these conversations and initial observations, I saw the significance of fast fashion as a nexus of several overlapping phenomena: just-in-time retail (more on what this term means below), automated worker scheduling, digital surveillance, precarity, policing, worker resistance, and labor organizing, to name a few.

Over the course of the next few years, I took a step back from teaching to immerse myself in the world of fast fashion. I returned with new eyes to the stores I once patronized, this time as a researcher attuned to the taken-for-granted processes underpinning the then-booming industry. I became a retail job applicant, an entry-level employee at two different companies—which I will call McFashion and Style Queen—and a volunteer with a retail labor workers' organization. I attended industry trade shows to observe how tech companies marketed their latest retail management and surveillance products. For personal stories and context, I interviewed fast-fashion retail employees, retail labor organizers, and activists. (For a longer description of my research methods, see the appendix.) My intention was to better understand and provide an on-the-ground account of the social forces that shape life and labor in the twenty-first century, and ultimately learn from workers and organizers on the front lines of imagining and pursuing more equitable horizons.

Throughout my journey, I kept coming back to one central question: How do technologies associated with fast-fashion retail exploit workers in new ways, and how are workers fighting back?

What I found was striking. Many of fast-fashion retail's core processes—including identifying consumer trends, deciding which garments to produce, and managing and scheduling in-store employees—have become automated. But contrary to many popular depictions of automation, robots have not yet eliminated retail jobs. Instead, low-wage clothing retail—already considered by many to be a "bad job"[1]—has become even worse.

Through observations, interviews, and firsthand experience, I saw how digital technology is deeply transforming the low-wage service sector. To be hired, job applicants must demonstrate total schedule flexibility and a willingness to endure chaotic working conditions. Once hired, automated schedules wreak havoc on employees' personal lives and health. While on the clock, daily tasks of frontline employees have moved steadily away from interactive service, resembling more and more the rote labor of Amazon fulfillment centers. Meanwhile, an array of digital technologies—which workers may or may not be aware of—track employee attendance, performance, and, to a certain extent, their lives outside work. Some of these tools were initially created for law enforcement and the military, while others developed in retail settings are being adapted by police. Yet whether individually or collectively, workers and their supporters challenge the new status quo, undermining and calling into question the pervasive use of digital monitoring and surveillance.

This book presents one of the first ethnographies of the fast-fashion retail industry, but perhaps more than that, this book is a firsthand story of work and life in the digital age. Until now, most accounts have centered on explicitly digitized and app-mediated lower-wage jobs. Amazon tends to dominate, and for good reason: employees there have been pushed to physical extremes, denied bathroom breaks, and had their every movement within the warehouses tracked, measured, and evaluated.[2] We also know that Uber has transformed the taxi industry[3] and that Big Tech companies are often powered by a vast, invisible network of "ghost workers."[4] Occupations like fast-fashion retail, outside the spotlight of Big Tech, often get left out of the conversation.[5] Here, too, technology has deeply transformed work, but perhaps in ways not quite so obvious as at Amazon or Uber.

When researchers *have* examined fast fashion, they haven't often considered the experiences of people who work inside the stores. Instead, most accounts focus on the labor conditions of garment workers as well as on the environmental consequences of constant consumption. This book thus also aims to shift the analytic focus of the retail industry from the *shop floor* to the *sales floor*. Ultimately, taking fast-fashion retail labor seriously allows us a deeper understanding of the many ways digital technologies have infused and transformed work and the broader social landscape.

The title of the book, *Worn Out*, refers to the consequences of a data-driven industry built on disposability. Fast fashion creates garments that quickly wear out and require replacing. As we'll come to see, many fast-fashion retail employees are also treated as disposable; they, too, are worn out. While many employees turn over and are replaced, others attempt to fight back. Historian E. P. Thompson once wrote: "The historical record is not a simple one of neutral and inevitable technological change, but is also one of exploitation and of resistance to exploitation."[6] That exploitation and resistance to exploitation, evolving in this digital age, is a central focus of this book. Along the way, I trace the sometimes invisible or unintended consequences of these digital management and surveillance tools, the landscape in which the companies that develop these tools operate, the many ways that workers experience the increasingly digitized workplace, and the linkages between worker and anti-surveillance organizing.

The "future of work" is not some moment in the far-off future; it's unfolding in the present moment. I hope this book might better prepare us—meaning retail workers, students, scholars, policy makers, labor organizers, and anyone else reading this book—to bend that future, to refashion it, toward one of justice and equity.

Outline

I begin the book by providing some context. In chapter 1, "How Fashion Became Fast," I describe how just-in-time manufacturing and reliance on big data distinguish fast fashion from other forms of clothing retail and allowed it to rise to prominence. I then review fast fashion's role in the global garment industry and situate fast fashion within the history of retail labor in the United States. Finally, I explain the political and economic role fast fashion played where I conducted most of my research: New York City.

Chapter 2, "Algorithmic Scheduling, Unstable Lives," describes various ways that retail employers use data and surveillance technologies to control workers' time outside work. Scheduling software uses sophisticated algorithms to help retailers cut labor costs but creates stress and unpredictability for staff. Because schedules vary so widely, total schedule flexibility has become a central hiring requirement, even beyond sales experience or loyalty to the brand. Employers weed out applicants through unpredictable hiring processes, pushing them to extremes even before being on the payroll.

Chapter 3, "The Automated Heart: Digitization of Service Work," takes us inside the store, where I show how the presence of digital surveillance technologies has radically altered the retail labor process. Service work used to be defined by a "managed heart" requiring routinized emotional labor of employees. In fast fashion, the work of knowing the customer has been automated. Digital tools can now track and predict consumer preferences at unprecedented scales. This change means the day-to-day tasks of frontline workers are increasingly focused on managing things rather than engaging with shoppers. I describe how at four zones—the stockroom, sales floor, fitting room, and cash register—workers must actively neglect interactive customer service to juggle the speedy flow of garments and maintain the appearance of the store. While automation has not yet eliminated in-store employees, it has intensified the physical demands of the job and increased worker anxiety.

Chapter 4, "How Retailers Use New Technologies to Surveil Workers," begins with ethnographic observations at a "loss prevention" conference, where retailers go to buy the latest surveillance technologies. Back inside the fast-fashion store, I find that automated scheduling systems encourage additional forms of digital worker control, from biometric scanners to cashier tracking. Alongside the demise of interactive selling, I observed the presence of another kind of emotion work—that of laboring under vast, and often invisible, digital surveillance. I call this the "emotional labor of surveillance."

Chapter 5, "Retail Disruptions: Confronting Digital Surveillance," zooms out to consider how the story of fast-fashion workers relates to broader social movements. I draw on my participation in and interviews with key activists in two social movements that created a political presence in and around retail spaces between 2014 and 2017—a workers' center called the Retail Action Project (RAP) and the Black Lives Matter (BLM) movement. These two movements, while employing at times vastly different tactics and demands, open space for *critical data praxis,* in which movements organize around the role of technology in perpetuating inequalities. This concept is rooted in the scholarship of Simone Browne and Ruha Benjamin, both of whom write about how technology has always been intertwined with power. By analyzing retail labor and anti-police violence movements together, we see how data travels across social contexts, and how movements might work together for collective liberation.

In the conclusion, I summarize how digital tools play a central role in disciplining fast-fashion labor, reinforcing economic insecurity among marginalized populations and entangling with more overt forms of state surveillance and violence. I consider what fast fashion teaches us about the future of work, and I offer readers suggestions for how they might take action.

1
How Fashion Became Fast

When I began my research, fast fashion felt sort of like the McDonald's or Walmart of clothing retail. Zara, H&M, and Forever 21 popped up throughout New York City while department stores and "slower" retailers struggled. Take Macy's Herald Square at 34th Street in Manhattan. The largest department store in the United States, it is, or was, a retail institution and department store par excellence. The eleven-floor historic landmark is known not only for its high-quality goods and superior customer service but also for its centrality in the holiday shopping season. The Macy's Annual Thanksgiving Day Parade is one of the largest in the world; the store's elaborate holiday window displays line 34th Street, a destination in and of themselves; and the location served as a backdrop for one of the most famous Christmas films, *Miracle on 34th Street.*

Despite its beloved status, the company's outlook was grim. In early 2017, the chain announced it would shutter nearly seventy stores nationwide and lay off almost 4,000 workers.[1] And Macy's wasn't alone. Payless, The

Limited, Wet Seal, JCPenney, American Apparel, Guess, and Sears were just some of the many retail companies closing hundreds of stores, if not liquidating altogether. Analyses from *The Atlantic, Business Insider,* and the *Financial Times* dubbed this the "retail apocalypse" and blamed the mass closings of department and branded apparel stores on the rise of online shopping[2]—"people simply buy more stuff online than they used to."[3] But this explanation fell flat to me. While most brick-and-mortar retailers struggled, another form thrived: fast fashion.

One needed only cross the street to see the distinction. On May 20, 2015, the world's largest H&M opened right there in Herald Square. Thirty-Fourth Street already housed two other H&M locations, just a few blocks east and west in either direction, meaning that in this stretch of the city, the retailer's density surpassed even Starbucks.[4] Nearly 10,000 people RSVPed on Facebook to H&M's flagship ribbon cutting ceremony, which included performances by music star John Legend and cash prizes of up to $1,000 to the first thousand shoppers. The store also offered 20-percent-off coupons to any customer who brought in a bag of recyclable clothing—a devious ploy that attempted to convince customers their addiction to shopping did good. (In fact, less than 1 percent of the collected garments are reused; the rest go to landfills or incinerators.[5]) The grand opening was scheduled to begin at 12 p.m. By 11:26 a.m., one hopeful attendee commented on the Facebook event page: "I wanted to go so I can get a gift card & give it to person as a bd [birthday] gift but I guess there's already the first 1000 people." The event epitomized fast fashion's mission: enticing a gigantic crowd into a celebration of ever-more continuous consumption.

I couldn't attend the grand opening in Herald Square, but I stopped by the store during its first Black Friday sale that November. I had spent most of the day participating in a "march of shame" with the Retail Action Project, where we picketed outside some of the busiest stores in Manhattan, amplifying workers' struggles on this day of unquestioned consumption. After the march dissipated, my curiosity about the new fast-fashion goliath got to me. *What was it like in there?* I wondered.

When I went inside, I noticed the store seemed busy but, to my surprise, not substantially busier than usual. I learned that in fast fashion, busy *is* business as usual. I wandered around, trying to peruse each of the four floors. Circling each level required maneuvering around overflowing tables and garment racks stuffed to the brim. Workers and shoppers engaged in an ongoing tussle: employees attempted to keep the store organized while shoppers rifled through the mounds of stuff. I overheard two young workers with the phrase "gift advisors" scrawled across the back of their black T-shirts commiserate about how exhausted they were.

I crouched on the third-floor balcony next to the live DJ, peering down at the main floor below and through

Figure 1.1
H&M Herald Square.

the glass walls to the street outside. Both were bustling with people, and police vans lined the surrounding intersection, a testament to the state's investment in protecting capital, especially on this most sanctified shopping day. As I glided down the escalator toward the bottom floor, dizziness washed over me. Light bounced off the mirror-lined ceilings, and I began to feel as if couldn't tell up from down (see figure 1.1). I wondered if this feeling was all part of the plan: good deals lure customers in, while the store's design—at first enticing but soon disorienting—pushes those customers out in due time, making room for a new batch of patrons desperate for a good deal.

To understand what brought the industry to that moment, it's helpful to put fast fashion in a political economic and historical context.

At the time of my study, fast fashion was an increasingly important player in the global market. I was stunned when I reviewed a list of the world's wealthiest people. Alongside Bill Gates and Jeff Bezos sat people like Amancio Ortega, founder of the multinational behemoth Inditex, parent company of the fast-fashion giant Zara. Also on the list was Stefan Persson, the main shareholder of H&M, a Swedish clothing store found in almost every major city in the United States.

In 2017, Forever 21 committed to adding 600 stores globally in the next three years,[6] and Zara and H&M each aimed to open 300 and 390 stores in 2018, respectively.[7] In the same year, even the big-box retailer Target had entered the fast-fashion game, aiming for monthly rather than quarterly garment deliveries.[8]

By 2021, as I write this book, the outlook for fast fashion isn't quite so rosy. In the fall of 2019, Forever 21 declared bankruptcy and announced it would be closing nearly 200 of its U.S. stores.[9] I address some of these more recent changes (due in major part to the COVID-19 pandemic) in the appendix, but for the most part, this book presents a snapshot in time, when fast fashion was at the cutting edge of retail labor. Fast fashion dominated, but surrounding stores closed one after the other. Signs reading "everything must go" were commonplace.

How did fast fashion become so successful? For one, the industry relies on and turbocharges 24/7 consumption.[10] On average, people own 400 percent more clothing today than they did twenty years ago,[11] expecting nothing from the retail experience *if not* a bargain.[12] Shoppers don't feel so bad tossing out a piece of clothing because it cost them only a few dollars. Consumers have been trained to access the latest trends for lower and lower prices. The rise of social media has only increased pressure to wear and display the latest styles.[13] By the time a trend has faded, the garment has likely already worn out and consumers are ready to purchase something else. During my research, I purchased a pair of jeans from one of the stores where I worked. A few months later, I hopped on my bicycle and the jeans ripped horizontally across the thigh. I didn't even know that was possible, but I knew that at $10, I couldn't expect much more.

In addition to changing consumption patterns, to really understand this industry, one must look at production. Fast fashion spearheaded the pace at which retailers design, produce, circulate, and sell their products. Whereas traditional branded retailers or department stores receive large shipments of garments a few times per year, fast-fashion stores receive inventory a few times per week. Daniel Kulle, president of H&M North America, said, "As we continuously are producing and having new item styles coming into fashion, we are replenishing *every day*."[14]

Fast-fashion retailers have benefited from, and pushed forward, a so-called global logistics revolution, in which the production and circulation of goods across the supply chain occur faster and more cheaply than ever before. According to industry experts, fast fashion represents the "long-awaited realization" of *just-in-time* production in clothing retail.[15] Department stores like Macy's or branded retailers like Abercrombie & Fitch long relied on a *push* model of production, in which factories sent retailers large shipments of clothing, which stores would then push onto customers through sales and coupons over the course of a few months.

Fast fashion and other just-in-time retailers instead participate in a *pull* model of production, in which data—such as that shared from retailers' sophisticated point-of-sale system (which is essentially a fancy cash register)—helps calculate exactly *how much* of each product should be replenished and *when*. Another way of putting it is that the push model focuses on producing large collections, whereas the pull model focuses on producing clothing at the item level. Staple or basic items might be produced with longer lead times in locations like Bangladesh, while trendier pieces are often manufactured closer to the company's "home"; Inditex, Zara's parent company, runs garment manufacturers in Morocco near its Spain headquarters, while Forever 21 produces some of its looks near its headquarters in Los Angeles. As a result of this "dual supply chain," trendy styles hit the sales floor quicker than ever.

This approach to retail supply-chain management was perhaps first perfected by Walmart,[16] but the advantages of just-in-time fast-fashion retail became truly evident in 2015. That year, the *New York Times* reported of retailers suffering through an unseasonably warm winter. Customers simply weren't buying heavy winter coats and bulky sweaters. The only companies that were able to "weather the weather," so to speak, were those in fast fashion, which could quickly respond to unexpected shifts in consumer demand, stocking stores with lighter-weight garments.[17]

Fast Fashion and the Global Garment Industry

While providing consumers with more affordable trendy clothing, fast fashion was embedded in a global garment industry that has exploited workers across the supply chain.[18] Over the past several years, journalistic exposés have revealed exploitative and often deadly working conditions within garment factories.[19] Most well-known is the 2013 Rana Plaza Collapse in Bangladesh, which killed over 1,100 people.[20] Several multinational retailers signed an accord to improve conditions, but developments several years later remain lackluster at best.[21] In Cambodia, H&M's garment workers have experienced mass fainting and are regularly fired for becoming pregnant, among numerous other "violations."[22] Several Cambodian garment workers have been killed in clashes with police following demands for higher wages.[23] In Istanbul, Zara customers found garments with messages sewn into them: "I made this item you are going to buy, but I didn't get paid for it."[24]

Garment workers struggle in the United States, too. The 2007 documentary *Made in L.A.* follows Forever 21 garment workers—many of whom are undocumented—in Los Angeles as they fight for fairer working conditions and higher pay.[25] These campaigns, while inspiring, have not always resulted in long-term structural changes. In 2016, the U.S. Department of Labor investigated seventy-seven Los Angeles garment manufacturers that served retailers including Forever 21, Ross (of the Ross Dress for Less brand), and TJ Maxx.[26] Eighty-five percent of the manufacturers violated labor laws, and some workers were paid as little as four dollars per hour. Advocates say retailers demand low prices from manufacturers and are thus directly implicated in labor violations. Yet retailers have faced no legal repercussions in these cases. As retailers source their items from an increasing number of manufacturers, we can expect these issues to continue.

Fast fashion also hurts the planet. A 2020 report argues that because retailers outsource so many aspects of their garment production, each product comes with a huge carbon footprint. In fact, retail is purportedly one of the largest contributors to greenhouse gas emissions.[27] By quickening the pace of production, fast fashion intensifies the environmental harms of the clothing industry.[28] Garment production is also water- and chemical-intensive, and washing certain fabrics like polyester releases microfibers into the earth's water supply.[29] In recent years, advocates have found "millions of tons of textile waste in landfills."[30] According to the U.S. Environmental Protection Agency, in 1960 people living in the United States generated 1,710 tons of textile waste; in 2018 that number had exploded to 11,300 tons.[31] In an attempt to save face, major fast-fashion companies increasingly attempt to brand themselves as environmentally conscious, a move that some critics have labeled "greenwashing."[32]

So far, I've described how fast fashion utilizes digital tools to speed up production, which has negative consequences for garment workers and the environment. If we hope to fully understand this industry, and to ultimately change it (or, indeed, abolish it),[33] we must take seriously how it impacts workers across the supply chain, including those inside its stores that line urban streets and have taken over shopping malls.

A Very Brief History of Retail Labor

From my initial observations of fast-fashion stores and conversations with employees, I could tell that working in these spaces was its own unique form of exploitation—sped up, focused even less on customer interaction, and digitally managed more than ever before. Research into the history and sociology of retail labor confirmed my suspicions. What retail labor looks like has shifted as retail companies and stores have themselves evolved.

The early twentieth century saw the rise of department stores, where staff could rarely afford the goods they sold.[34] A department store sales associate might have lived in a small, cramped apartment with family or friends. But at work she had the chance to rub elbows with the upper middle class and to be surrounded by glamour and fashion. She prided herself on knowing about the products she was selling and the people she was selling them to. That was part of the allure. She might not make much money, but a full-time position might allow her to pay her bills, and perhaps even buy a few of the items she herself sold. Of course, those who were hired had to at least *look like* they belonged in the store. For the most part, major retailers preferred to hire people who embodied white, middle-class aesthetics. Other employees remained relegated to stocking, cleaning, or other back-of-house duties.[35] For these reasons and others I'll discuss later in the book, retail was a central site of struggle for the twentieth-century civil rights movement.[36]

To a certain extent, this dynamic remained true with the development of branded retailers, like Victoria's Secret, The Gap, Express, The Limited, and others. Employees were incentivized to work for minimum wages through special discounts[37] and association with the company's brand[38] or customer base.[39] In other words, even if employees were poorer than most of the clientele, they might get to *feel like* part of that store's world just by working there.

As the retail industry evolved over the twentieth century, so too did the nature of work. Beginning in the 1970s, jobs in the Global North became increasingly feminized and insecure, regularly lacking benefits, decent wages, or union representation.[40] Compared to the stereotype of the post–World War II era, in which workers often possessed "lifetime" careers as embodied in the "organization man" wedded to the company,[41] today, people regularly cycle through many jobs throughout their adult lives.[42] In retail, nearly 60 percent of workers are hired on a temporary basis, and the median duration of employment for part-time retail workers is just one year.[43] Turnover can have especially detrimental consequences for people on the lower rungs of society, living paycheck to paycheck.

Working in twenty-first-century fast-fashion retail, I would come to learn, is different from working at department stores like Macy's or even branded retailers like The Limited. At the time of my study, more important for applicants than "looking good and sounding right" was having an open and flexible schedule; these jobs are increasingly part-time with ever-changing hours and zero benefits. One report found that between 2003 and 2013 "the number of involuntary part-time workers has more than tripled."[44] Instead of developing knowledge about the products they sold, today's retail workers succeed through speed and efficiency. Interactive customer service has taken a back seat to processing incoming shipments of new items almost daily and maintaining a hectic sales floor where items are so cheap, they practically sell themselves.

Today's retail industry is certainly more diverse that it once was. A 2014 survey found that 62 percent of retail workers are women, and 21 percent are people of color.[45] At Walmart, for example, women comprise 55.7 percent and people of color comprise 26.4 percent of hourly workers.[46] In contrast, the U.S. general population in 2014 was comprised of 51 percent women and 38 percent people of color.[47] At first glance, it therefore would seem women are over-represented and people of color are under-represented within the retail sector. Yet compared to other retail sectors (such as grocery stores or general merchandise), clothing, shoes, and accessories retail employs 73 percent women, by far the highest percentage of women in the retail workforce,[48] as well as the highest portion of Latino workers (23%) and the second-highest portion of Black workers (13%).[49] The think tank Demos reported in 2015 that Black and Latinx retail workers are more likely to live in poverty, work in part-time and on-call positions, and remain in low-paying and entry-level positions.[50]

When I first began my research, I was unable to find demographic data on the fast-fashion sector specifically. My educated hunch, based on extensive fieldwork, was that fast-fashion retail workers were some of the most exploited in the industry and comprised a high portion of society's already marginalized populations. Most fast-fashion workers I encountered in New York City were women, queer people, and primarily Black and Latinx. In nearly every group interview I attended, I was one of just a few white applicants out of twenty to forty people. Of the twenty retail workers I formally interviewed, twelve identified as women, trans, or non-binary; eighteen were people of color; and two were white.

In recent years, a few major fast-fashion retailers have shared figures in "diversity, equity, and inclusion" reports, perhaps as a response to the global uprisings against racism and police brutality. Inditex reports that Zara's in-store retail workforce was 79 percent women in 2017. A recent H&M report says 25 percent of its retail workers are Hispanic or Latinx and 20 percent are Black or African American; meanwhile, just 13 percent of managerial workers are Hispanic and Latinx and 6 percent are Black or African American.[51] These figures support my educated guess: the retail workforce in general is a highly feminized and racialized one, and fast fashion even more so.

Yet inclusion in an exploitative industry might not be a good thing. A 2014 report by the Retail Action Project based in New York City reads: "Retailers' demands for open availability and the use of unpredictable scheduling means that workers already struggling with low wages and discrimination in our economy—women, people of color, caregivers, and lesbian, gay, bisexual, transgender, and queer workers—are left in a constant state of insecurity."[52] Activist-scholars Amber Hollibaugh and Margot Weiss use the term "queer precarity" to explain how these working conditions compound the insecurity already faced by marginalized populations.[53]

These trends were no truer than where I grounded my research: New York City.

New York: Fast Fashion's Flagship City

Manhattan is home to many of the largest fast-fashion retailers in the world. New York City is in many ways the industry's *flagship*: if a shopper wants access to the biggest, most heavily stocked, glitziest fast-fashion stores in the United States, if not the world, then New York City is the place to be. Zara set records in 2015 when it purchased space for its newest location in Manhattan's SoHo district for a staggering $280 million, or nearly $20,000 per square foot.[54] In Herald Square sits the world's biggest H&M. Less than ten blocks north in Times Square, tourists flock to the world's largest Forever 21, which opened in 2010 and spans an astonishing four stories. These giant stores have become a destination for tourists; families planning to see a Broadway show and visit Times Square may go inside Forever 21, if for no other reason than to marvel in its gigantic glory.

In the city that never sleeps, even fast-fashion stores are open nearly around the clock. Before I started research for this book in earnest, I took a trip to Times Square one snowy Tuesday a little after 11 p.m. Although having grown up in the Midwest, in Iowa, I was no stranger to fast fashion. My only disposable income as a teenager came from my part-time jobs working for minimum wage at ice cream stores, hair salons, and daycare centers. If I wanted new clothes, my favorite destinations were Goodwill thrift stores and Forever 21. But these stores I had grown up with had limits. All items were crammed onto one floor, and the mall never stayed open later than 9 p.m. The thought of being able to go to a fast-fashion store in the middle of the night, during the week, and having multiple levels of clothing to choose from felt weirdly exhilarating.

When I got off the train and walked toward Times Square, the glowing lights disrupted my senses, making me feel more awake than when I began the journey. Looking back at photos I took outside one storefront, I noticed how difficult it was to discern the time of day. Inside, the store was gleaming. Upon entry, I passed by a guard standing watch. Quite honestly, he looked bored, but nevertheless his presence reminded me that someone was always watching. Further inside, I felt disoriented by the space's vastness. I would wander around and forget what I was doing, or why. I would hum along to a song because it was so loud I couldn't hear myself think. Suddenly, I would find myself in the underwear section for the second time, not realizing I had already made multiple trips around the perimeter of the floor. Part of this disorientation came not only from the music and the enormous amount of inventory, which began to blur together, but from the lighting and displays. Light bounced off the white flooring, mirrors, and metal clothing racks. I felt like I was in a fashion funhouse.

At the same time, I felt surprised by the sense of normality. As it turned out, shopping there at 1 a.m. feels a lot like shopping there at 1 p.m. Customers browsed as employees organized disordered purses and hauled clothing racks across the floor. I asked one employee how they were doing. "Tired!" They said had just come from their other job. "This is my life!" they added with a smile, sweeping their arm like Vanna White along two racks of jackets. I asked if they knew a former student of mine who worked at this location. "Mmm nah." "How many people work here?" I asked. They raised their eyebrows, trying to calculate. "I dunno, maybe hundreds." On the way out, I struggled to remind myself: this experience felt might have felt somewhat normal, but only because I lived in a place and a culture that normalized constant work and constant consumption.

Coincidentally, while I waited on the platform for the train heading back to Brooklyn, I overheard a conversation between two H&M employees. One person complained about enduring a closing shift, and their coworker exclaimed, "That's what open availability means! I get a lot more morning shifts, but doing display, I still have to close." As I observed, creating this world of always-available consumption required a lot of workers. And the more I looked out for it, the more I saw fast fashion throughout the city. Several of my students and acquaintances worked in the industry; encounters like the one above with workers were not uncommon; and people carrying the telltale sunshine yellow Forever 21 bags or white and red H&M shopping bags caught my eye on nearly every train ride.

On my way home, I thought about Manhattan's history. The city hadn't always been a 24/7 tourist destination. As described so beautifully in Samuel Delany's book *Times Square Red, Times Square Blue,*[55] if previously rife with crime, the Times Square of earlier decades was in some ways more alive, a place for locals, artists, rejects, and weirdos to hang out, meet up, and go to the movies. My night in Times Square in the twenty-first century looked much different, mostly comprised of international tourists and people on their way home from work. It was as if Times Square's tourism makeover included corralling locals indoors as low-wage hourly employees.

The sanitized look and feel of much of New York City is the result of specific kinds of collaborations between government and business. For example, at the time of this writing, the area of Union Square houses Forever 21 and Urban Outfitters, as well as H&M nearby. A Business Improvement District (BID) collected extra property taxes to "clean up" the neighborhood, making it welcoming to businesses and appear safe to consumers.

Sociologist Sharon Zukin argues: "Most important, if rarely stated, these associations work to raise property values in and around public spaces, which cannot be done if homeless men and women sleep on park benches, muggers threaten shoppers, walls and lampposts are covered with graffiti, and cities fail to provide the basic services of street cleaning, trash collecting, and policing on which the urban public, including the businesses that rent commercial real estate, relies."[56] To achieve these urban makeovers, BIDs rely on a combination of digital and analog (i.e., not digital) surveillance, including local police, neighborhood watch people, closed-circuit television (CCTV), and an evolving array of high-tech apparatuses.[57] Redesigning Manhattan's landscape into a beautified shopping destination infuses the fabric of everyday experiences and opportunities of people living in New York.

It only made sense that I would conduct my study in what is ostensibly the world's flagship city of both "high" and "low" fashion.

When I share this research, some people ask me what distinguishes the world of fast fashion from a retailer like Walmart. In this study, we can look to the relationship between the corporations and the broader urban landscape. There are no Walmarts in New York City—although its e-commerce site, Jet, leased a warehouse in the Bronx in 2018[58]—whereas fast-fashion retailers are sprinkled across major urban centers. If Walmart dominates suburban and rural landscapes,[59] fast fashion dominates suburban and urban ones. Fast fashion is thus more closely linked to urban networks of surveillance and policing.

As I'll describe throughout the rest of the book, my coworkers and interviewees possess intimate knowledge of these geographies. They've watched the working-class families, workers, and artists get pushed out of Manhattan or rendered invisible by giant chain stores. They've observed surveillance cameras and police protect the giant corporations that employ them. And many have experienced these same places come alive in protests and efforts to create change.

2

Algorithmic Scheduling, Unstable Lives

I interviewed twenty-one-year-old Derek in my apartment. It was a Sunday morning and he had spent much of the previous night out with one of my roommates. I was impressed by how alert he seemed on so little sleep. But perhaps I shouldn't have been surprised. I would come to learn that Derek was used to operating on just a few hours' rest. Derek had been working at Zara in Manhattan for six months. He made $12.75 per hour. It was tough, he told me, but better than his other job at a Duane Reade drug store. One recent evening, he was scheduled to work at Zara until store closing at 10 p.m., yet he and his coworkers didn't get out until midnight. In New York City, the subways run less often between midnight and 6:30 a.m., so Derek waited, exhausted, on the sweltering subway platform before catching his train to Port Authority Bus Terminal. Then he waited again for his bus to fill up for the ride back to New Jersey where he lived with his cousin. He didn't get home until 1:30 a.m. He was scheduled to work the next morning at the drug store at 6 a.m. Buses don't run that early, so Derek walked to work at 5 a.m.

Believe it or not, Derek was one of the lucky ones: few retail workers felt as if they were "allowed" to have more than one job at a time. Because fast-fashion retailers want their employees to have "open availability," they are told they can have only one job, even if it's part-time and doesn't pay the bills. For a few months, Derek juggled two. He eventually quit Duane Reade, in part because he made $1.50 more per hour at Zara. "I couldn't deal working two jobs anymore."

Even with just one job, Derek, like many other fast-fashion retail workers, felt as if he didn't have a life. He told me Zara was supposed to post employee schedules two weeks in advance, "but in reality, it's like two or three days." Although fast-fashion retailers rely on the latest technologies, most of them still use a decidedly old-school method of posting employee schedules, often just a piece of paper tacked to a bulletin board in the break room. When I first started working in the industry, I would make special trips and spend $5 in subway fare just to check the schedule. But Derek and his coworkers had a system. They created a text loop where one person would take a picture of the schedule and share it with everyone else in the group. They utilized their own devices to make their lives easier. Still, making plans was nearly impossible. "My friends will ask me, what's your schedule next week? And I have no idea."

The only time Derek felt financially secure was right after payday. That feeling didn't last long. "If I got paid last Friday," he told me, "I'm not going out this Friday because I can't afford it. I've got another week to get through." He said it would be easier to get by on what he was paid if he was better at saving. He couldn't resist Dunkin Donuts coffee. "I could never give that up!" I told him that's not that much money and he deserves a coffee and a donut to make it through his shifts. He felt even more guilty about the pair of shoes he just bought, but he had valid reasons for dropping sixty bucks. The shoes Zara had given him as part of his uniform caused him back pain. The black Vans he wore now were much more comfortable. Without a doubt, Derek's biggest expense was transportation.

I asked about the Fight for 15, which, at that time, had made significant headway into raising the minimum wage for fast food workers, but was struggling to apply those changes across the board for all workers. Derek said, "I've heard of that. That [$15 per hour] would be wonderful actually, because, like, that would make a lot of our lives so much easier. Sometimes it's hard to live off of $12.75. If I had *real* bills to pay, I couldn't do it. With what I make? A person can't survive off that." I wondered if Derek worked at Zara *because* he had no "real" bills, or if working at Zara *prevented* Derek from taking on "real" expenses, such as going back to school or moving out of his cousin's place.

Over the course of my project, Derek became what sociologists would call one of my "key informants." In other words, he was one of a small handful of people I regularly consulted with about this project. I knew

Derek through my roommate, and I conducted a formal, in-depth interview with him. The formal interview supplemented several other lengthy, but more informal, conversations. He came with me to meetings at the Retail Action Project (RAP), a worker's center that I'll discuss more in chapter 5. We even took a day trip together with RAP to Albany, in Upstate New York, where we gathered with other unions and labor groups to pressure state lawmakers to extend $15 per hour to all workers (not just fast food workers). I'd been worried Derek was bored by hours of standing listening to speeches, but he later told my roommate, "That was so cool!" and "$15 an hour, yes please!" Derek might have been my "informant," but he was also my friend.

Overall, Derek's story helps illuminate one of the central conflicts of fast-fashion retail: cutting-edge technologies help fast-fashion corporations rake in huge profits, but, clearly, these tools are almost always used in the *employers'* interest. Meanwhile, employees jump through hoops, such as having to check their ever-changing schedules that are posted on a piece of paper. Unpredictable schedules plus low wages make Derek's life outside work chaotic and hard to plan. At the same time, we see how Derek and his colleagues, in creating and updating their own text thread with the employee schedules, draw on their own devices to perform labor even after they clock out.

This chapter looks at how technologies control workers' lives outside work. I begin by describing automated scheduling software, and I show how flexible schedules add to the stress of low-wage retail labor. Automated flexible scheduling has become so central to how fast-fashion stores operate that it has even impacted the interviewing and hiring process. Employers have long used pre-employment assessments to screen job applicants;[1] now, the ability to endure erratic scheduling and to demonstrate open availability has become a pre-employment assessment of its own.

Tools of the Trade

Before looking at today's digital tools and what they might portend for future workers, it's useful to take a glance back.

In the early twentieth century, working in retail meant working long, insufferable hours. As historian Susan Porter Benson describes: "At Macy's, sitting while at work was forbidden and 'unnecessary conversation' could lead to instant dismissal. Hours were long, stretching to sixteen hours per day in the busiest seasons; employees' facilities were unsanitary and even squalid. Low wages were the scandal of the industry, and even further reduced by fines which placed 'a value upon time lost that is not given to service rendered.'"[2] The labor movement fought for an eight-hour day through much of the late nineteenth and early twentieth century. In fact, the central demand of the first-ever May

Day demonstration in Chicago in 1886 was for an eight-hour workday.[3] After continued struggle and incremental progress across individual industries, the Fair Labor Standards Act of 1938 limited the length of the working day to eight hours; otherwise, employees should receive overtime wages. The FLSA covered wholesale sectors but did not apply hourly standards to retail until 1961.[4]

Today, some department stores, such as Macy's, pay associates based on commission. With a commission structure, associates are paid based on the amount that they sell. The more they sell, the more money they take home. Commission can be especially attractive at department stores that sell high-end and luxury goods; that could be one reason that some employees stay at places like Macy's for decades. In fast fashion, low wages remain a "scandal of the industry." Now, in addition to wages, low-tier retail workers confront another problem: instead of working *too many* hours, they often work *too few*, and with little to no stability in their schedules or paychecks. Many Fight for 15 rallies I attended featured signs like: "15 & Full-Time." Indeed, higher wages meant little if bosses cut hours.

Flexible scheduling carries profoundly negative consequences for low-wage hourly workers, who come to shoulder the risks and instabilities of the market. If the store sees fewer customers, workers see fewer hours and smaller paychecks. It's incredibly difficult to support oneself, let alone other people, under such circumstances. For example, let's say a retail employee, whom I'll call Alex, has a two-year-old child and works a flexible schedule. Alex takes their child to a nearby daycare and then drives across town to their job. Some days, when the store is slow, Alex is sent home early. Other days, when the store is busy or a coworker calls out sick, Alex is asked to stay late. Their kid's daycare closes promptly at 6 p.m. and fines parents who are late to pick up their children. Alex is lucky enough to get off at 6, but they must race over in their unreliable car that may or may not break down. If Alex lived in a bigger city, they might rely on public transit, which itself is often unpredictable. Finding someone else to pick up Alex's child on short notice can be difficult; they receive their schedule just a few days in advance and sometimes is called into work the same day. Some weeks Alex is scheduled for thirty-two hours' work; other weeks they are scheduled for just eight hours across two shifts. Unpredictability makes it difficult for Alex's family to establish a routine and pay their bills. The ever-changing work schedule is an added stress on top of low wages, lack of healthcare, and everything else that goes along with being a low-wage worker in the United States. This is just one example of how flexible scheduling is almost never designed with workers' interests in mind. On top of that, the scenario doesn't consider the exorbitant cost of childcare.

A growing number of scholars document these challenges in detail,[5] but they rarely discuss the role of *technology* in making these conditions possible. In the previous chapter, I discussed how fast-fashion retailers use just-in-time production and big data to know exactly how much of which item to produce and when. This orientation is part of what made fast fashion so wildly successful. Employers have taken a similar approach to scheduling. Along with *just-in-time inventory,* fast-fashion retailers have harnessed digital technologies to achieve *just-in-time labor* in which employee schedules parallel shopper traffic.

One of the most well-known third-party companies attempting to automate workplace management across a number of industries—including retail, health care, and even law enforcement—is called Kronos. Their website features a link to a "Time and Attendance Solution Guide" in which readers can "learn how automated time tracking improves daily operations, cuts payroll waste, and creates a culture of compliance." With the help of this software, retailers can track vast sets of data that allow them to align employee scheduling more closely with consumer demand.

Images from Kronos's website provide some insight. Figure 2.1, for instance, illustrates the variables that might go into a scheduling algorithm: "Working with the historical data from your point-of-sale (POS) system—items such as units sold, customers, transactions, traffic, and sales—Workforce Forecast Manager predicts weekly business volumes using the amount of historical data you have available."[6] The predicted weekly business volume then shapes the employee schedules.

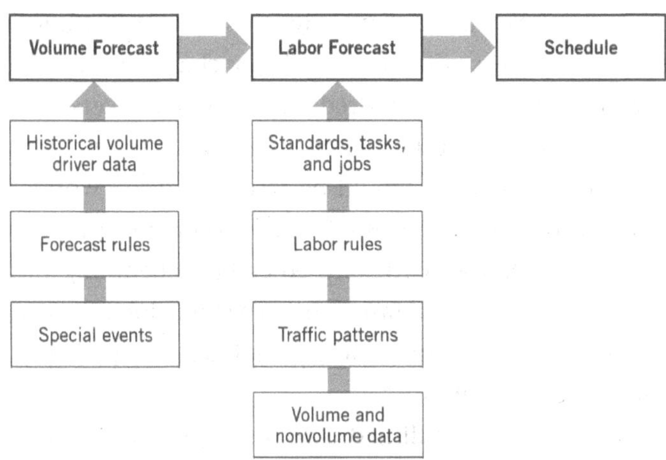

Figure 2.1
Kronos workforce scheduling algorithm. *Source:* Kronos.com.

That might seem simple. But as journalist Esther Kaplan reports, algorithms used by Kronos and other companies can be more complex than initially meets the eye: "Scheduling software systems, some built in-house, some by third-party firms, analyze historical data (how many sales there were on this day last year, how rain or a Yankees game affects revenue) as well as moment-by-moment updates on the number of customers in the store or the number of sweaters sold in the past hour or the pay rate of each employee on the clock—what Kronos, one of the leading suppliers of these systems, calls 'oceans of valuable workforce data.'"[7] Notably absent from these "oceans of data" are needs of employees.

Kronos claims their workforce management platforms leads to "higher satisfaction for employees and managers." Yet, as Kaplan writes: "In August 2013, less than two weeks after teen fashion chain Forever 21 began using Kronos, hundreds of full-time workers were notified that they'd be switched to part-time and that their health benefits would be terminated."[8] I wonder if, as Kronos claims, those workers experienced higher satisfaction. Since 2013, unpredictable scheduling has become a norm in fast fashion; not a single job I applied to offered full-time positions, yet all desired applicants with "open availability."

Automated scheduling did not come out of nowhere. In her 1993 book *Fast Food, Fast Talk: Service Work and the Routinization of Everyday Life*, Robin Leidner describes how McDonald's relied on "highly specialized equipment" that "calculated yields and food costs, keeps track of inventory and cash, schedules labor, and breaks down sales by time of day, product and worker."[9] At the time of her writing, schedules were allocated in thirty-minute increments. Software like Kronos draws on the ethos of fast food—uniformity, efficiency, routinization, and speed—and bring it into the era of *big data*, which some have described as "vast, fast, disparate, and digital."[10] Kronos is like the "specialized equipment" at McDonald's on steroids: it analyzes much more data, from a wider variety of sources, at a quicker speed. Kronos claims it can calculate schedules in as little as fifteen-minute increments.

When I was researching this book, one of Kronos's newest products was called Artificial Intelligence for

Managers and Employees, or AIMEE: "AIMEE is on the job even when you aren't. Always working behind the scenes to solve problems and provide advice on critical decision-making. So your business can run with the intelligence and efficiency all employees expect of today's technology. With AIMEE, managers and employees spend less time looking for the story and more time focusing on delivering great outcomes for their customers."[11] When industry leaders talk about *the future of work*, they are often thinking of tools like AIMEE. Big data, automation, and artificial intelligence are leveraged to optimize performance and boost profits.

Algorithms might not have entirely eliminated the role of humans in crafting schedules, however. Here's how one human resources manager I interviewed, Heaven, explained it:

> We—including HR, the commercial and financial teams—all get together with the directors. We start analyzing based on the increase [in sales] they want for the next year. Once commercial has finalized that version of the budget they send it to HR. Based on this amount, what we do is we look at the past year and then we look at the hours [that] were given to them [employees]. And what we do is pretty much try to balance everything with what we call a productivity target. And try to balance out based on the sales what hours work best to have good productivity.

In the workforce management dashboard shown in figure 2.2, and as explained by Heaven, labor hours are always measured in relationship to labor cost. Giving

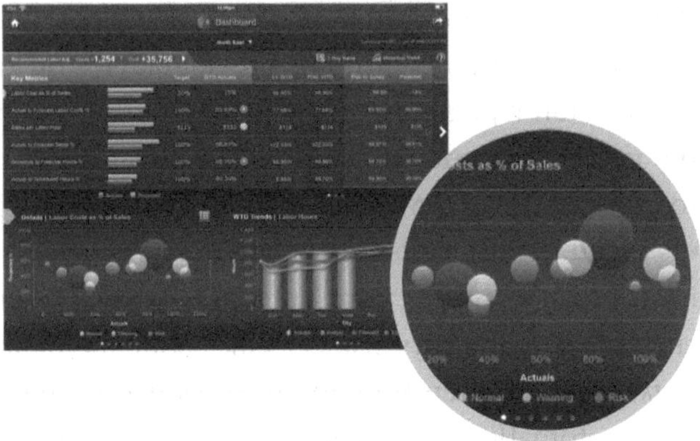

Figure 2.2
Kronos workforce management dashboard. *Source:* Kronos.com.

workers too many hours if sales are doing poorly would lead to a "bad productivity" ratio. Heaven told me that managers would sometimes exceed their "budget" for hours, and HR would have to step in:

> I tell them they have to go to next week's schedule and reduce fifty hours from the entire schedule. So, the schedule shifts. We pretty much give all the part-timers twenty hours. That's the minimum we as a company provide. Twenty hours. But the full timers are at forty. Sometimes if they need to reach those hours full-timers drop to thirty-eight hours. Also, what we do, we have managers ask, "Does anybody wanna go on vacation?" If it's very critical we start asking part-timers, "Is there anyone that would like to take unpaid days off? And enjoy the weather?" We do that as well. That's how we recover.

Heaven's account echoes a job advertisement I came across for a "Kronos & Timekeeping Administrator" with a "Fashion Industry Company" on an online job board. The position summary reads, in part: "Position will maintain employee schedules in Kronos and partner with operations on identifying employee behaviors in compliance with the Reliability Policy." While this all sounds somewhat reasonable, implementation of this process can have detrimental impacts on the lives of frontline employees.

Just-in-time production and data-driven retailing may conjure images of well-oiled machines, of total and harmonious synchronization between computers, human laborers, and consumers. The reality, I discovered, is much messier. What I found highlights the enduring contradictions of contemporary capitalism in which high-tech efficiencies exist alongside, and in fact deeply rely on, the inefficiencies and daily anguishes of low-wage work.[12]

Automated Schedules, Unstable Lives

What do the demands for total flexibility look like for workers? Many frontline workers I interviewed told me that they verbally communicated their scheduling needs to their managers, only to be seemingly ignored. To begin with, workers are told that fast fashion is their primary job. This happened to me at Style Queen.

During my final interview, I asked, "If I were to get another part time job, would y'all be able to work with me in balancing the schedules?" "Nooo," the manager replied. "Since this is retail, we need you to be available Friday, Saturday, Sunday, plus two weekday closing shifts. If you're in school we can work around your class schedule, but that's it." I found that so interesting. If Style Queen could accommodate school schedules but nothing else, that means they weren't *unable* to accommodate scheduling needs. They were simply *unwilling* to do so. Where did that leave people who had kids or other caregiving duties? I heard rumors of some workers who were able to sneak in a second job, like Derek at Duane Reade or one of my Style Queen coworkers at Starbucks. But most had the lesson drilled into them. As one person I interviewed repeated: "This is your primary job, even if you only get fifteen hours a week. Don't tell us you have to work a shift somewhere else because in your contract this is your primary job." This is your primary, low-wage, unpredictable job.

At both fast-fashion retailers I worked at—McFashion and Style Queen—employees were scheduled to work at all hours of the day, some arriving as early as 3 a.m. to help process incoming shipments, others staying as late as 4 a.m. to help close a store. "They want it, like, perfect in the morning," one worker, Kya, told me. Another employee I interviewed, Jayla, couch-surfed with her friends to cut down on transportation time. My coworkers chugged coffee and Red Bull to make it through the early sprees processing clothes in the stockroom, sometimes making themselves sick. While Style Queen posted its schedule one week in advance, we were lucky to have just a few days' notice at McFashion. For many, then, the only constants were uncertainty and exhaustion.

Hours varied so much that even the most assiduous workers lost track of when they were and were not on the schedule. During one of my first shifts at Style Queen, I was mentored by David, a longtime sales associate who regularly trained new hires. That evening, a manager approached us, clipboard in hand, to check in. At the end of our conversation, he said to David, "Okay sounds good. You leave at 8?" "No, 6," David said confidently as he leaned against a garment rack. "Says here 8," the manager replied, showing him a copy of the schedule. "Well, I'm gonna go check in back. I swear it said 6." David returned a few minutes later, admitting his mix-up. This was the first time I'd ever seen him in the wrong.

Following legislative action and widespread disdain, many retailers have ceased on-call scheduling, but workers still have no idea when they'll be asked to come in. During my month-long tenure at Style Queen, I was called and asked to come in that same day at least three times. Each time I said no. My manager, Dante, would quip, "I hate you!" and hang up the phone before I could respond; he would also approach me while I was at work and ask if I wanted to stay late. Although technically voluntary, he would be visibly disappointed when I would deny the request. "I'm just trying to pay your bills!" he would shout. While I don't doubt Dante's intentions, Style Queen frequently presented itself as having its workers' best interests at heart. Calling people in at the last minute and asking them to stay late isn't helping people. What would help is offering people higher wages and stable schedules, with flexibility that could be used to accommodate *workers'* needs. At the end of the day, the retail industry and companies like Style Queen, with the help of third-party platforms like Kronos, were responsible for our exploitation.

Sara Sharma uses the term "time work" to talk about how precarious workers must attune their daily rhythms to the demands of others.[13] Sharma profiles taxi drivers who wait around for their next customer and then race their passengers to the airports. In New York City, fast-fashion workers too must attune themselves to the constantly shifting pace of modern retail. Near the employee schedules posted in the break room of most stores, you'll see white sheets of paper, either taped to a table or tacked to a wall, where workers scribble their names and numbers if they "want more shifts" or if they have a shift they're looking to give away (see figure 2.3). Long-term workers were well adept at this game; retailers are known for drastically cutting shifts of more senior workers while continuing to bring on new hires.[14] Private Facebook groups, or text groups like Derek's, allow workers to swap shifts or post schedules

Figure 2.3
Analog "time work."

online. These strategies are a critical piece of "time work" when employers sometimes post the schedule as little as a day or two in advance of the coming week.

As I anticipated, the constant vacillation of worker schedules infused workplace relations. I was shocked that even those in power had difficulty keeping track of employees. Managers regularly forgot when I had clocked in, and my coworkers taught me to advocate for myself when my break was due or my shift over. Near the end of one of my training shifts, David told me to take my fifteen-minute break. "But the manager told me at the beginning of the shift I shouldn't take a break since I'm only here for four hours," I said. David responded, "Don't ever let them tell you that! Don't worry. I'll tell the manager you're going on your fifteen." I was grateful someone was watching out for me.

I heard of similar issues during interviews with retail workers. I talked with Ryan on a warm summer day at an overpriced sandwich shop in midtown Manhattan. Ryan had black framed glasses and smiled a lot. He had attended SUNY-Buffalo and the Fashion Institute of Technology for a few semesters. He wasn't sure if he would return to FIT in the fall or go back to Buffalo. One thing he did know for certain: he was getting tired of working in retail.

Ryan was a full-time employee, but here's what he said when I asked him about his schedule: "On average they try to do like twenty hours, thirty hours, maybe even forty if they like you on the floor. Most of the time I'd say between ten and twenty." In other words, Ryan was full-time, but worked anywhere between *ten and forty* hours per week. Most people would have a difficult time building a life around that kind of schedule.

Later in the interview, he told me categorizing people as full-time felt to him like a "scapegoat." What I think he meant was that the designation was a shallow title with nothing to back it up. "The new workers, they're full-time too but they get part-time hours. So, it seems like they work their way into [full-time]. But then again when you first start you get full-time hours, but then after two weeks you're like, 'I was maxing out. Now I'm doing like fifteen. What happened?'" I had felt this too. It seemed like there was no rhyme or reason to how many hours we were scheduled. And often it created tension among coworkers, since almost everyone needed the hours and the money.

Luckily, the company Ryan worked for had recently halted on-call scheduling after widespread critique by local labor groups. Ryan told me the on-call scheduling simply didn't work. "It came to a point where people weren't working. People were like, why should I even work if I'm not really gonna work? Like, okay, I have thirty hours a week but fifteen of them are on-call. If I don't take any of those on-calls, I just made, like, what $150 for the week?! And you're like, this is ridiculous. A lot of people quit for that." According to Ryan, his company halted on-call scheduling not because it was unfair to workers, but because it led to high turnover. So, when it didn't work *for the company*, the company halted the practice.

Sometimes scheduling conflicts led to workers being disciplined or fired. One person I talked with, Rachel, worked at Zara in Los Angeles for nine months. As we spoke at a Starbucks on the Upper West Side of Manhattan, she told me that she disliked how working in fast fashion made her feel like "just another body." When I asked her to clarify, she told me the following story:

When I was fired, I guess I felt that a lot. Because it was a very weird situation. I got an opportunity to work a trade show for a week and it was gonna be a really good opportunity for me. It was a lot of money, and for half of the time I was not working. But I had two or three shifts I couldn't make because of this because I was out of town. So, it was the week before and I tried to get people to cover. But I couldn't get anyone to cover my shifts. I looked my manager in the face, and I asked him, "What should I do?" And he said, "Well, you know, we'll just have to see how it goes." And I was like, "That's not an answer."

So, I specifically told my assistant manager Michelle who I was really close with. And she and I had a really good relationship. And I looked her in the face and said, "I am not coming these three days because I have another commitment. Like, just so you know what's going on." She was like, "Okay." So, I leave. That's the last word I get of it.

I come back. I pick up my paycheck. I try to get my next schedule. She was like, "Oh I need to talk to you outside." She pulls me aside. And she was like, "You didn't show up for work three consecutive days without calling out, so that means you officially gave notice." And then I was like, "What?! Like, are you kidding me?" I understand, but at the same time, I told my manager and my associate what was going on. I said if you just told me I needed to call in I would have done that. You know me. I've been here nine months. I'm not the type of person to just leave without any warning. And so I felt very, like, I dunno, like I wasn't explained my rights kinda thing. And I wasn't really fully informed.

Though Rachel described feeling like "just a body," to me, it also seemed as if she was just a data point. Maybe this is what Esther Kaplan meant when she called her essay on data-driven management "The Spy Who Fired Me." Despite what seemed to be open communication and reasonable expectations, Kronos or a similar program might have flagged Rachel's absences as "out of compliance" and she was fired. Here, the human in the data is lost. The company's bottom line succeeds, and workers' lives suffer.

Total Flexibility

Employability in the data-driven retail sector relies on demonstrating total flexibility. Even more surprising than what happens to seasoned workers, I found fast fashion places temporal demands on job applicants far prior to their first shift.

McFashion

I began applying for fast-fashion jobs in June 2015. Since I was undercover (for more information about what this means and the ethical implications, see the appendix), I feared being outed, but I also questioned my ability to hack it even if everything went according to plan. Despite my working-class roots, service labor has never been my strong suit. To assuage my fears, I undertook some pre–job application sleuthing by doing what all rigorous academics do: I turned to Google. A search for "job interview McFashion" generated their listing on Glassdoor.com, a website where employees rate and describe their experiences working with employers. I learned many employees had applied online first, so that's what I did. At the very least, I figured an online application would help me gain familiarity with the application process; I had witnessed in my previous ethnographic project how job searching was almost always also a practice of self-making, and this proved no exception.[15] The web portal asked typical questions about my work history, and since I had negligible clothing retail experience, I practiced sculpting my history into something mildly relevant. I played up my time as a volunteer sales associate at Bluestockings, a feminist bookstore in Manhattan. I also listed my recent internship at a local book publisher, highlighting my marketing experience and the fast-paced nature of the work.

After several days without response to my online application, I stepped things up a notch, deciding to go into the store during one of their biweekly job fairs (an early indicator of the workforce's constant churn), where they were hiring for sales associates and overnight stockers. According to a Glassdoor testimony, one applicant had recently gone to this same location for the very same job fair, only to find that none of the employees had even heard of such a thing. Disorder, I expected, was the norm. My interviewees had

had similar experiences. Ashley, someone I interviewed who had worked at Zara, wasn't surprised that it took her over a month to get hired and that her application had been lost in the process: "I had heard that unorganization [*sic*] was, like, a continuous thing."

I arrived at McFashion around 6:30 p.m. on a Monday evening. Getting there was its own adventure. Times Square is almost always jam-packed with ogling tourists with several children in tow, street performers in grimy Sesame Street and superhero costumes, and disgruntled workers trying to maneuver their way back to the office. In the sweltering summer heat, the wafts of air conditioning escaping from McFashion's revolving doors lured me inside, where black-suited guards stood silently by the entrance. The blasting pop music drowned out the sounds of the crowds, and the grit of the street stood in stark contrast to McFashion's gleaming linoleum floor, tall white walls, sparkling chandeliers, and artfully displayed bright clothes. While things looked good from a distance, close-up everything was a mess. Garments were strewn over clothing racks and sometimes entire racks had been knocked on the floor.

I headed down three flights of escalators to the bottom floor, and after waiting in line behind a few customers, I asked the cashier for a job application. He couldn't find one but asked to see my resume. "They're going to stop doing interviews soon and I happen to be a supervisor. Do you have experience?" he asked. "I have some retail experience. I've worked at a bookstore but never in fashion." He reviewed my application. "Give me five minutes. Let me get my manager. You seem like a good candidate." I moved to the side so other customers could continue to check out; meanwhile, another employee brought me an application, which I began to fill out. I saw the supervisor walk back over with his manager, Stacey, with braids that hung just past her shoulders and a flannel shirt tied around the top of her perfectly ripped jeans. After the supervisor told Stacey I might be a good candidate, she looked me up and down, presumably judging my aesthetic fit with the job. "Okay," she said positively, and motioned me to follow her. She reached her hand back behind her as she walked. "Resume. You got one?" I handed it to her, realizing she had mastered the art of multitasking, surveilling the store while simultaneously judging my fit with the job.

Then, abruptly, we stopped. "Let me ask you this. Have you ever been to this store?" she asked skeptically. Oh no, I'm blowing it! I thought. Maybe I should have omitted my teaching experience from my resume. "Yeah, McFashion is actually one of my favorite stores."

"Really." The skepticism in her voice was clear.

"Yep, McFashion, Style Queen, and thrift stores are where I shop most."

"Okay. And what times have you been to this store?"

"Various times, actually. I've been here in the late afternoon, late night."

"Good, so you know how busy it gets."

"Yes, and actually I know someone who worked here before, so that's why I considered applying."

"Okay, go find a place to sit by the escalators. Finish filling out your application and I'll go get you some paperwork."

After at least twenty minutes, I started to wonder if Stacey would ever come back. When I saw her reappear, I followed her to the dressing rooms where she addressed the staff. I smiled and attempted to hand her my application, thinking that would be the end of it. "I still need to get your paperwork. I didn't forget about you!" I sat back down, waiting another ten minutes or so before she returned, and I followed her to the escalator. "Are you another interviewee?" Stacey asked another woman. The woman said no, but I didn't think too much of it.

"You sure you still wanna work here?" Stacey asked as we reached the intimates section. "Yep!" I replied. "Just checking," she said. "Wait here." She went into a back office and returned with a stack of papers, which she placed on a display table among piles of frilly undergarments and pajama tops. She walked me through the packet, highlighting what I needed to fill out, when suddenly she yelled hello to a young woman walking by. "Do you still work here?" Stacey asked. "Um, yeah!" the young woman replied with a laugh. I was starting to identify a pattern, in which even managers struggled to keep track of employees.

Stacey told me to expect a phone call from her the following day to arrange a time to return to the store.

"So I should be prepared to come in to interview?"

"No darling, there's no interview. You're hired."

"What's your name again?" I asked as she escorted me out. She extended her hand and gave me a firm handshake. "Stacey. Nice to meet you."

Even as I thought I was on the fast track, I encountered serious bumps in the road. By the following Tuesday, I still hadn't heard from Stacey, so I called the store, finally reaching someone after twice getting busy signals. Stacey was not in that day, but the person on the phone took my name and number and claimed someone else would call me back that night or the following day. When I hadn't heard anything by 7:30 p.m. on Wednesday, I called again. When no one answered after six minutes of being on hold, I hung up and called back. This time someone else told me orientation was tomorrow at 11 a.m. but said that if no one had called and told me that, then I wasn't eligible. I felt confused and frustrated. I said Stacey had hired me and given me the new hire packet, but she simply never called me back. They then told me that I *was* hired, but they needed to put my information in the system first, which can take anywhere between two weeks and a month.

On Thursday morning, I took the hour-long subway ride back into the city, my completed employee information packet in tow. I was directed to the lingerie section, where about thirty young applicants stood in a steadily growing line. "I hope this doesn't take long," one person said. Another asked, "Do you think we get paid for this?" Two people behind me had already turned in their paperwork; one said it took McFashion a month to get back to them, another said two weeks. Finally, an employee emerged from the office, and I asked her what I should do with my packet. That employee waved down a manager, who said she couldn't deal with me right now, but could I come back at 10 a.m. Monday morning? I told her I could and asked her if I would be doing orientation then. She told me no, that it would take a few weeks, but I should bring in a copy of my passport or driver's license and social security card.

That morning, I had spent over two hours and five dollars in subway fare just to get sent home. This waiting time is crucial; not only does it delay the period between application submission and start date, but it requires new employees to put in unremunerated labor of repeatedly traveling to the store and bearing the costs of childcare and transportation. Research has shown that pricey commutes disproportionally affect the poor.[16] At the time of my research, a single ride cost $2.50; it increased to $2.75 in March 2017. As sociologist Javier Auyero writes in his study of welfare recipients, and as sociologist Pierre Bourdieu documents of medical patients, waiting is a tool of governance, the "exercise of power over other people's time both on the side of the powerful (adjourning, deferring, delaying, raising false hopes, or conversely, rushing, taking by surprise) and on the side of the 'patient' as they say in the medical universe, one of the sites par excellence of anxious, powerless waiting."[17] "Anxious, powerless waiting" was a regular experience in my fast-fashion job search.

I returned the following week to submit my paperwork, finding the store surprisingly calm upon arrival. This should be a quick process, I thought to myself. I made my way down to the office. I was stunned to see that, like last week, a line of people preceded me, this time about twenty deep. Around six were men, and I was the only white person. I approached the woman at the back of the line, and I saw the manila folder in her hand, as well as in the hand of the woman in front of her. A wave of relief rushed over me: I was not the only person submitting paperwork. I hoped I was at least in the proper place this time.

After ten minutes, a woman approached the line and told us that the operations manager was running late—he had been stuck on the train for an hour and a half. She then gave us each a slip of paper with a number on it so that we could step out—use the restroom, get a drink—and not lose our place in line. I took the opportunity to leave the store to get a coffee, letting the sugar coat my sore throat while I considered the irony of the situation. I wondered if such leniency would be applied to employees who were late because of the train. This temporal regime was another opportunity for the chopping block; if applicants were late or missed one round, they were out of luck. Jayla, who had worked at another McFashion location, shared a similar experience:

> At first you have to do a group interview and then they narrowed it down to smaller groups at first. Yeah, you did a group interview first. Then once they picked you from that point, it was like you were kind of hired but they were still kind of testing you. You had to go in and learn about the stores. A lot of people did drop out, those little training sessions. Because for whatever reason they couldn't make it. And it was kind of like if you couldn't make it, then we uh, you know you weren't gonna make it into the store. So, you did the group interview, they picked the people from there, you did a few training sessions. If at any point you were late or whatever, you weren't working there.

When I returned fifteen minutes later, the operations manager had just arrived and took in the first five applicants. In total, I waited two hours for my turn. As Jayla noted, it was like a test: if we couldn't make it through this time discipline, there's no way we'd make it as employees. The stakes became painfully clear when an older applicant, who had difficulty standing for long periods of time, was chastised by a passing security guard for resting on one of the display tables. "That's for clothing only." Indeed, precarity is felt deep in the body.

Finally, around 12:15, it was my turn to go into the office with four other women. We sat on metal folding chairs, huddled around the table. "How are you ladies doing? Thank you for waiting." The operations manager, Chris, was quite charming, but also had a sternness to him; he reminded me of an affable gym teacher on the first day of class, who would soon show his true colors once the semester started. He took our IDs and social security cards. "Does anyone know why we're all here today?" A woman to my right said, "To hand in our packets?" to which Chris laughed. "That's not the only reason, otherwise we wouldn't have you wait for so long. This is what we call your information audit. It's not orientation, which confuses some people. What we're doing today is going through all your paperwork line by line to make sure you have all the necessary information there. Because after you hand it in, I'm going to input it and submit it to corporate, and if you're missing a signature somewhere, I'm going to have to call you and have you come back in to sign it. And that's not any fun for anyone. For some people it's a trek just to get here. So today we're making sure you've got everything you need as quickly as possible so we can get you out enjoying this beautiful day." As usual, the strict rules of the store were framed as promoting workers' best interest, without acknowledging the role of the company in creating these conditions of insecurity.

Before we left, Chris told us the next step was to be called back for orientation. "It will take anywhere from two to three weeks. Sometimes less, sometimes more. One guy turned his paperwork in on Monday, was called back on Tuesday, and came in for training that Thursday. So be ready, and answer your phone, 'cause I do *not* email." Already, I had been into the store three times, waited unexpectedly for hours. I felt like I was on call.

I couldn't make any travel plans, or indeed any kind of plan, not knowing when the training would occur.

My orientation occurred one full month later, in July. In my case, I was happy for the month-long waiting period. My sore throat that morning turned into a case of strep. Without health insurance or access to proper medicine, it seemed to last forever. Meanwhile, I moved into a new apartment after my previous building had caught fire. Given everything that was going on, if I had been hired at McFashion on the spot, there's no way I could have made it all work, especially given their strict attendance policy. But for others, going a month without a paycheck would have been impossible.

These early encounters with McFashion presented early lessons in fast fashion and job seeking. Proving oneself employable meant demonstrating not identification with the brand, as might be common in other retail contexts,[18] but, more importantly, comfort with chaos—a flexible, anonymous, and disposable subjectivity in the service of capital. In their analysis of luxury retailers, Williams and Connell warn of the shuffling schedules that await newly hired workers, writing, "In addition to being subjected to long waits, retail workers rarely have control over their schedules *once they are hired*" (emphasis mine).[19] However, I found that the demands of open availability began far prior to the official start date.

As I advanced toward paid employment, I experienced how precarity unfolded across perceived categories of difference,[20] with my whiteness easing my efforts. At one point, I shared with my friend Emma, a Latinx labor organizer and former retail worker, about how I was hired on the spot at McFashion. I said it "was probably just because I'm white." Emma responded, "Right, I was thinking that, but didn't want to sound racist. But those places do like to hire white people." Of course, Emma was not the racist one; the companies were. In the appendix, I discuss more about how these power differentials solidified my commitment to using this project to support and amplify efforts to improve retail working conditions.

My next round of job hunting was even more dramatic.

Style Queen

By the next spring, I had quit McFashion but was looking to reenter the job market. I walked up and down Broadway in SoHo one dark, rainy evening, asking nearly every clothing store if they were hiring. A small, more traditionally branded retailer nearly hired me on the spot, while another fast-fashion company sent me through the loop. I attended an open interview, then received a voicemail that the next in-person interview would be rescheduled. I called back the number on the voicemail, but got only an automated message. I went into the store two days later and was told I missed the interview. After talking with a manager, I was finally let into another interview. I thought it went well and wrote in my notes how I was legitimately excited to work at this store. Still, I heard nothing. "You have to really hound them," Emma advised me. Apparently. I was getting worried about paying my rent and wrote, "I feel so defeated, or at least worn down. I've been in there so many times before. I am begging for this job."

At first, Style Queen, seemed more promising. The store associates told me the best way to apply was online, and after doing so I received a call-back just two days later. "This process seems like it will be so much easier!" I wrote in my notes. Yet when I tried to return the call, it went straight to voicemail. Here we go again, I thought. Thankfully, someone answered the second time I called. I was able to schedule an interview, but not until three weeks later. Anxiety set in as I knew my bank account was dwindling.

By the time the first interview rolled around I had almost forgotten about it, in part because I was still chasing a job at another retailer. The Style Queen office on Broadway looked modern but worn down, and was partitioned into three sections: a waiting room, a conference room, and an open meeting room with large bay windows. Small bags of chips and miniature bottles of water sat in the middle of the table. This was a step up from McFashion, which conducted the interviews inside the store's shopping area.

Eight other applicants joined me that day, far fewer than what I had experienced at McFashion, perhaps because these were by invite only. These interviewees dressed more conservatively; most of the women wore all black, while the men donned button-ups and slacks. We were guided into the meeting room, where four different Style Queen employees asked us questions. The questions foretold the nature of the work that awaited us:

What's a time you had to deal with a difficult customer?

What's a time you had to make do with few resources?

Tell us about a time you had to complete a project with a deadline, and what was the result?

When is a time you had difficulty with a coworker and how did you handle it?

From these prompts, I gathered that working at Style Queen would be fast-paced, stressful, and tense. For the most part, I was right. But this was only the first round of interviews.

The following week, I returned to the Style Queen SoHo office for a second group interview. I thought perhaps I was interrupting a meeting when I saw so many people in the waiting room. One of the interviewees piped up: "It was really cold out today, right? I thought it was gonna be warm but I was freezing when I took my kids to school." It was the first time I heard anyone mention having kids. I wondered how she would manage it.

Joe, whose slicked-back black hair matched his black outfit, announced with the cadence of a game show host, "Okay, is everybody ready to get started? Are you all ready for a *fun* two, two and half hours? This is going to be like no interview you've ever experienced before. This is going to be an interactive interview. We're not just going to sit and ask you questions, you're actually going to get to see and experience what it's like to work at Style Queen, and we'll get to know a bit about you." Two and a half hours! I wanted to back out.

We were escorted to the main room where chairs were arranged in a large circle. Atop each chair lay a uniquely colored ribbon. We were instructed to creatively attach the ribbons to ourselves, and throughout the day we would be referred to by our ribbon color. I immediately tied my ribbon around the crown of my head like a headband, an instinct that I carried with me from my younger, more feminine self. I noticed the interviewers watching us and the interviewees watching each other. To my surprise, each person managed to come up with something different: one person tied theirs like a tie, another like a necklace, a bracelet, a pageant sash, a belt. I felt as if we were beginning a secret ceremony, a rite of passage. Little did I know, the next few hours would feel more akin to hazing.

With this first activity, the employer impressed on us the importance of our aesthetic labor. Even if we weren't going to be able to develop a knowledge of the products we were peddling, we at least needed to perform the fashionista role. If branded apparel companies seek employees who *fit in*,[21] fast-fashion companies recruit people who *stand out,* modeling for the customers as wide a variety of looks as the stores offered. There remain, of course, limits to marketable difference. For example, while certain forms of gender and sexual nonnormativity might be welcomed (evidenced by Zara and H&M's attempts to "break barriers" by venturing into gender-neutral clothing[22]), trans customers and workers continue to face discrimination.[23] And as my interview at McFashion suggests, hiring practices still privilege white applicants.

At that point, we were introduced to each of the interviewers. Joe had been with Style Queen five years. Anastasia, a middle-aged Eastern European woman, had been with Style Queen several years as the head of hiring. Dante, who would later be my manager, had been with Style Queen for only twelve weeks.

Then the games really began.

We split into two groups and followed Dante into what had been the waiting room, where we were instructed to move the chairs to the walls. Around the center table were three large plastic containers and a clothing rack. Anastasia told us she would give us directions for a task, and we could ask questions, but after she started the clock, we weren't allowed to ask any more. Dante, who stood in the corner with a clipboard, would be watching silently, taking notes. Anastasia explained that we were to unpack all the clothes, put them on the clothing rack, and make a nice display as quickly as possible. For this, we would have ten minutes total. At the same time, there was a piece of paper with a list of questions on it. Throughout the activity, we were to take turns pretending to be the customer by reading from the questions listed on the paper, asking other employees for help. It didn't matter if we knew the right answer, we were told, just be as courteous as possible.

"Ready, go!" We all rushed to the boxes and began unpacking. I grabbed a handful of green flannel shirts and flung them on a hanger. "Make sure they look nice!" Anastasia warned, so I fumbled with the buttons, fearing I wasn't moving fast enough. "Where's the customer? I don't hear the customer!" Anastasia shouted. We took turns yelling customer questions into the melee, waiting for someone to answer. *Where's the bathroom? Can I return this? Where'd you get your pants? Can I keep the hangers?* Anastasia snaps: "I don't see a neat display! You have six minutes left!" A herd of us rushed over to the table, attempting to straighten the garments. Everyone was panicking, talking across each other. Anastasia: "The manager called, she doesn't want any jeans on the table!" We started hanging the jeans on hangers. Anastasia: "Where's the neat display? I still need a neat display! I want to see a nice outfit on the table!" I asked the woman next to me: "So then we can have one pair of jeans on the table for the outfit, right?" As she rushed to put a shirt on hanger, she responded, panting, "I don't know, she said no pants on the table." Was this a job interview, or retail boot camp? It felt as if Anastasia was our abusive parent, and we were her children, too scared to make a wrong move, but also too meek to ask questions. I resigned to the fact that she would never be satisfied. "Only one more minute left!" Thank god.

"Okay, time's up!" We all stood around the table, smiling and fanning ourselves to cool down. "In one word, what are you feeling right now? Let's go around." Anastasia pointed: "You." *Tired. Hot. Excited.* I said, "Invigorated," attempting to put a positive spin on it.

"Do you think this is how Style Queen works?" she asked.

Was this a trick question?

Anastasia: "I hear some people saying yes and some people saying no. Well, no, we won't have managers yelling at you to change something this quickly, unless maybe there's a sale going on. You *will* be expected to juggle many things at once, but our customers should always remain our top priority. Okay, nice job everybody. You can sit down while we prepare our next activity." Anastasia's words made clear a central bait-and-switch of fast-fashion rhetoric. Official discourse continues to prioritize customer service, whereas the demands of the garments almost always take precedent. In the activity—and, as I would come to find, in the actual work—customer service was an impossibility, a literal distraction. We were to feign positive affect, but never were we to veer from our organizing tasks, nor were we encouraged to provide thorough and helpful answers to customer inquiries.

After a few minutes, we were steered into the other room, where several large cardboard boxes sat stacked against the wall. I assumed it was going to be similar to the last activity, but Joe instructed: "You are in charge of creating a window display for Style Queen's new line called 'woke wear.' You need to make sure your display conveys a clear message, is visually pleasing, and appeals to the brand's targeted customer, which is teenagers. Any questions?" I felt like a player in the Hunger Games, attempting to solve a challenge with our team members, all the while prioritizing our individual performance. After Joe yelled, "Ready, go!" we briefly strategized, but our plan soon evaporated. Upon moving the boxes, we discovered paper taped to two sides, which had up to that point remained concealed to us. Some papers had symbols on them (blue stars, red hearts, or green dots), while some had letters. The letters, we soon realized, spelled "woke wear." We arranged them in the middle of the room, attempting to make a visually pleasing display. Joe announced, "The manager called, and he actually wants the display against the wall." We all rushed to put the pieces against the wall while keeping the display intact. Another announcement: "I just heard from the manager, and they said we can't have any letters on the bottom of the display!" We rearranged the boxes, placing letters on the second layer. Joe: "Hey guys, the manager says no red stars on the bottom!" I could barely concentrate over the sound of boxes shuffling around.

"Okay, guys! Time's up!"

Once again, Joe asked, "How do you feel in one word?" This time, the responses took a negative turn. *Tired. Exhausted. Awake. Hot.*

"Can someone sell this display to me?" Joe asked. One applicant calmly explained this was our new look for spring, with stars for summer and green for our eco-friendly clothing. We all nodded, impressed. "And who is our customer?" "Teenagers!" someone shouted. "Good, you were paying attention. What did you find difficult about this exercise?" Joe asked. One person mentioned the confusing directions, someone else complained about the changing prompts, and I said I felt like we started out strong by strategizing but could have checked in with each other more throughout. "Keep these lessons in mind as we continue the interview." I sighed, exhausted.

While we were waiting (quietly this time; the excitement had worn off), Dante told us, "This next activity is what sealed the deal for me. I knew after doing this activity that Style Queen was different and I really wanted to work for them." The setup for the finale included three tables surrounded by chairs facing away from the tables. Atop each chair's seat was a Tupperware container full of toy blocks, and on the table sat a container of Legos. A Lego mat lay in the center of each table. There was also, inexplicably, a tennis ball.

This activity was the most complicated and, on the surface, least clearly related to the job. Each team was to collectively build a Lego castle, with each layer alternating colors, with one window on each side and one door. At the same time, we were to build towers on our individual chairs with the toy blocks. But that's not all. Finally, we were to bounce the tennis ball around the table in a clockwise direction. If at any point we dropped the ball, we were to shout, "STOP!" and all work should cease until the ball was put back in rotation.

After Joe shouted "Go!" I tried to yell to my teammates to devise a plan. But the sudden commotion made verbal communication nearly impossible. I heard Joe: "Keep the ball moving! Keep the ball moving! Keep the ball moving!" I felt as if we were starting to get the hang of it, then came another command: "You should be building a tower! You should be building a tower! You should be building a tower!" I couldn't concentrate. I tried to build the Lego castle with one hand and the toy block tower with the other. "Manager says no red Legos are allowed." Someone tore the whole thing apart and shouted, "Let's start over! Build a smaller tower, it doesn't have to be so big!" I had learned from the previous activities that anything we do will be wrong, so I thought I may as well just keep up the *appearance* of working. At one point, I started mindlessly attaching Legos to the castle and pretending to build a tower with the blocks on my chair.

"Okay, time's up!" How did we feel this time? No bones about it—not good. I said, "Sweaty."

Joe approached the other group. "What were the guidelines given?" Someone sheepishly responded, "It was supposed to have alternating colors." "And did you do that?" "No, but we do have the windows here and here," the applicant said, pointing. "So, you didn't follow directions?" "No," they responded, shamefully. Joe then approached our group and scolded us similarly. The lesson, we were told, was that at Style Queen, we would always have to balance multiple tasks. The Lego castle supposedly represented group tasks, the toy block tower represented individual tasks, while the tennis ball represented customers. Although they didn't say so, as in the first activity, the customer could never be top priority; they were merely a distraction to the more taxing demanding of handling and rearranging mountains of stuff.

We gathered all the materials and put them away, rearranging the room so all the chairs were around one long table. Joe said, "This was *fun*, right? Have you ever had an interview like this before?" Someone mumbled, "I never want to do this again." Joe asked if we had any questions for them. "Will there be another interview after this?" someone asked. "There could be a third interview yes." I felt my eyes bulge out of my head; I've never had a good poker face. Joe justified: "Style Queen is a difficult company to work for, and we want to make sure we select the proper candidates." Apparently, a proper candidate was one who could endure stress and humiliation with very little reward.

One applicant asked, "If we don't get a call-back this time, how soon can we apply again? 'Cause I applied to multiple stores, and the others told me to wait and see how this one goes." Joe explained, "The company will respect the decisions we make here across the board, so you need to wait awhile before you apply again. Maybe this time is not right for you, or maybe the positions were filled, or maybe you don't have the right kind of big box experience. So maybe you want to get a different job to get that kind of big box experience and then apply again." I thought of a commercial I often saw on late-night TV as a kid. It featured someone going through a revolving door saying, *I can't get a job without any experience. I can't get experience if I don't have a job.*

I had one final interview the following week. Dante called me and asked me to come into their Columbus Circle location. "This is the last step. I promise," he assured me. I should hope so! The next day I spent over an hour on the train to get there. When I arrived I was told Dante wasn't in yet. Hmmm. I returned to the store entrance and ran into Ariana, a red-headed woman who was interviewed at the same time I was. She was coming out of the back office and had spoken to someone who told her to come back at 2:30 p.m.

"She's going to be conducting the interview, but she wanted to wait till Dante was here," Ariana said.

"That's so weird. I could have sworn he told me 12:30."

"Yeah, he definitely told me 12."

"Uhm what are you gonna do until then?"

"I'm gonna walk around the mall, I guess! I told the woman it wasn't a problem since my mom's got my kid. I really want this job!"

I was happy Arianna had someone to watch her child. I felt bad that we had to try so hard for jobs that treated us, as Rachel had said, like "just a body."

Technology supposedly makes lives easier. But whose?

Workers on Demand

The extensive role-playing scenarios at Style Queen seemed outlandish to me, but based on a review of organizational psychology, what I experienced was in fact common. Psychometric tests—with names like "situational judgment" and "maximum performance"—are meant to measure fit with the job role, weed out poorly qualified applicants, and reduce churn, which can be quite costly for the organization. This literature even makes clear the importance of these assessments in balancing workers' roles "in customer contact and 'as factory workers.'"[24] Competing to stack cardboard boxes, racing to hang and re-hang clothes, and building Lego towers while bouncing balls around the table—all while being observed by the hiring committee—indeed tested our ability and willingness to endure the grueling and lightning-fast world of fast-fashion retail labor.

Some employers have attempted to measure job applicants' propensity for absenteeism. One questionnaire, called the "Dependability and Safety Instrument," measures factors like compliance—including "returns from breaks on time"—and dependability—defined as "rarely has time off" and "is always reliable."[25] I did not take any such questionnaire, but I didn't have to: the erratic scheduling of the interviews themselves weeded out potential candidates. Testing applicants' ability to put up with vague and often contradictory scheduling instructions, unpredictable wait times between multiple interview rounds, and last-minute requests was its own kind of maximum performance assessment, revealing just how much applicants would take.

Throughout the process, applicants learn to provide employers with complete flexibility. If applicants are hired, automated scheduling creates deep insecurity and unpredictability. This insecurity can be felt in the body, whether through the exhaustion of rushing to and from shifts, the adrenaline and sweat of enduring intensive job interviews, or a heart racing at not knowing when one's first paycheck will drop or whether it will be enough to pay the bills.

In this chapter, we've seen how technologies shape these low-wage workers' lives outside work and before being hired. Now let's look at life on the sales floor.

3
The Automated Heart: Digitization of Service Work

Sociologist Arlie Hochschild argued in her 1983 book *The Managed Heart* that service workers perform "emotional labor."[1] That is, in these sectors, the product being sold isn't a *thing*, but rather an interactive service or *experience*. To perform their jobs properly, service employees must mask and alter their true feelings. They must manage their hearts: you might have noticed this with flight attendants who smile politely at rude passengers, or fast-food workers who recite canned lines—*Would you like fries with that?* Even white-collar workers such as bill collectors put on a proper show, effectively "creating alarm" among debtors.[2]

At the time, Hochschild's thesis was profound. Few academics had considered the role of emotion in producing value. Since the release of *The Managed Heart*, the idea of emotional labor has become mainstream; the concept is now so well-known and widely used that some people say it's losing its original meaning. In common parlance, emotional labor now refers to any emotional work done in any context, including in family or intimate relationships. Hochschild reminds us in a recent interview: "Emotional labor, as I introduced the term in *The Managed Heart,* is the work, for which you're paid, which centrally involves trying to feel the right feeling for the job. This involves evoking and suppressing feelings. Some jobs require a lot of it, some a little of it."[3] So, in this chapter, I explore Hochschild's concept where she originally intended it: at work.

On the one hand, fast-fashion retailers are selling more items of clothing than ever, so one might assume that sales associates must therefore perform even more emotional labor. But that's not at all what I found. In fast-fashion retail, interactive service work—that is, the work of engaging customers—is now at the *bottom* of most workers' list of duties. It's not sales associates, but data analysts, who do the real work of getting know the customers. If in the 1980s, 1990s, and early 2000s, the retail worker's heart was *managed,* today, it's becoming *automated.*

An array of tracking software catalogues and predicts consumer behavior and desires.[4] Most of us are now all too familiar with personalized social media ads tailored to our internet browsing histories, and this data also influences what ends up in retail stores. Bloomberg Business reports that the secret to fast fashion's success is "more data, fewer bosses."[5] Digitized point-of-sale systems (which I'll detail more in the next chapter) and RFID (radio-frequency identification) microchips embedded in clothing track the amount and timing of items sold. This information is then fed back to corporate data processing centers where analysts gauge current sales and predict future purchasing behavior. Instead of packing huge warehouses full of items to be sold (i.e., the "push" model of production I mentioned in the chapter 1), this real-time, data-driven analysis of consumer desires allows fast-fashion retailers to replenish stock in quicker, bite-sized frequencies (i.e., the "pull" model of production). If, according to analysis, items sell well, the retailer can order more. If the items don't do well, it's not a huge loss.

Similar to how big data customizes, tailors, or personalizes other aspects of everyday life, big data in retail allows companies to customize inventory based on sales data from each location.[6] Jesús Echeverría, chief communication officer for Inditex (Zara's parent company), told the fashion website Refinery 29, "The commercial teams at our headquarters, which are in touch with every store location, [decide] exactly what to order for each store. Some stores prefer more denim; others want more suits."[7] Companies increasingly leverage online customer shopping and browsing information as well. Christopher Wylie—a data analyst and whistleblower who exposed the Cambridge Analytica scandal—said upon being hired as a research director for H&M: "We can't help people if we don't know who they are. With the use of data, we can make sure our customers get what they want."[8] By mining all this information, the goal is for customers to be able to get what they want, when they want it, at a price they can't refuse.

Some people say data analysts know customers better than customers know themselves. This leaves sales associates doing little actual selling.

Karen Levy and Solon Barocas call this phenomenon *refractive surveillance*: data collected about one group—shoppers—impacts the lives of another group—retail workers.[9] Levy and Barocas consider how retail's refractive surveillance can lead to unpredictable schedules like those I described in the previous chapter. Data collected about customer behavior also transforms the *kind* of work retail employees do and *how* they do it. Levy and Barocas say that new technologies could make workers more replaceable by digitizing customer service. In other words, employees no longer possess that oh-so-important information about consumer preferences and desires; instead, computers track it. That is certainly the case in fast fashion. Yet even as retail workers hadn't been entirely replaced, labor in fast fashion looks much different from that in other retail contexts.

It's easy to sense some of these changes from a consumer standpoint. As an adolescent in the 1990s, when my friends and I would go to the mall, we would sometimes play "The Buckle Challenge." The Buckle is a clothing store geared toward teens and young adults. Back then, it carried brands like Lucky, JNCO, Mossimo, and No Fear, and their sales associates were notoriously aggressive, which made my introverted pre-teen self panic. However, I did partake in a few rounds of the Buckle Challenge. Typically, the game was played with two or more shoppers who begin at the store entrance. Whoever could reach the back of the store and return to the entrance without being spoken to by a sales associate won. Come to think of it, I'm not sure I ever won. One thing I am sure of: attempting to play that game at a fast-fashion store would look much different.

Today, when one enters a fast-fashion retailer, one rarely interacts with a sales associate. In fact, customers often struggle to get an employee's attention. Scathing comments about the lack of customer service abound on sites like Yelp and Google:

> Longest lines, not enough employees, everyone you ask for help acts like your [*sic*] bothering them . . . ughhhh after shopping for hours I was very tempted to leave the line. Annoying store.

> One star is too generous. Stood in line for about 40 minutes, because there was only one cashier for a line that was all the way to the door. Store manager obviously saw the line but kept stepping to the back to hide from customers, absolutely useless. Had two other employees on the floor folding clothes, when they could've been more useful in helping at the register.

> Crowded, messy, and so busy the staff doesn't have much time to help customers. But cheap good looking clothes!

The trendy styles and low prices—made possible by leveraging data—make up for the lack of service. As I heard a few times throughout my research, the clothes are so cheap they sell themselves.

The reliance on digital technology to track consumer behavior, predict clothing trends, and produce clothes just as they're needed has led to notable trends in fast-fashion retail labor. The journey as I'll describe it begins at dawn, in the stockroom, where workers arrive early each morning to process incoming shipments and where fast fashion most explicitly resembles the factory. Once the clothes flow onto the sales floor, however, the work of "maintaining" the store and the stuff within it remains—against common conceptions of service work—a top priority. Sales assistants must limit contact with—if not actively avoid—customers to keep the floor in functioning order. When we peer into the fitting room, we see an astonishingly similar dynamic. Even as customers explicitly ask for help, workers must often deny it in lieu of "garment caring," or preparing the clothes for return to the sales floor—a revealing term indicating the true target of employee concern. Finally, chaos culminates at the cash register, where shoppers must decide, once and for all, if the deal of the day makes up for a lack of service and severely long lines.

Each zone of the store—stockroom, sales floor, fitting room, and cash register—highlights the unique characteristics of this latest iteration of apparel retail. The skilled selling of early department stores is nowhere to be found, and even the rote emotional labor of branded retail stores like The Limited or Abercrombie & Fitch has little place here. As we'll see, however, this transition from a managed heart to an automated one encounters frequently snags, with resistance from both customers and employees.

"The Heart of Our Store": The Stockroom

Given the centrality of producing and circulating garments with speed and precision, some of the most significant retail labor happens *off* the sales floor, in the stockroom. Stockroom associates occupy a crucial role in the company's success, connecting local stores with the global supply chain. With shipments arriving a few times per week, stock associates ensure new garments continually make it onto the sales floor. During my fieldwork, I came across this job ad for a stockroom associate:

> We are looking for a very energetic, hardworking, reliable and effective Stockroom Associate. We need a professional and detail oriented person with a sense of urgency and motivation. Our large stockroom requires a lot of time and dedication. It is the heart of our store! We receive large shipments twice a week with different garments and we need to price them, organize them, and sensor them in a very effective and FAST way.

From this quote, we learn that stock associates, not often seen by shoppers, work in "the heart of the store," the pulse that keeps the garments circulating, without which the store could not survive. At McFashion, associates were hired to work primarily in the stockroom, while Style Queen trained associates "globally," in which all entry-level workers rotated working in the stockroom, on the sales floor, in the fitting room, and at the cash register.

Not surprisingly, working in the stockroom feels most explicitly like being in a factory. With its dull cement floors, towers of plastic bins, and austere plastic tables for processing clothes, the stockroom offers none of the glitz and glam of the sleek shopping area just a few feet away. There is no pulsing soundtrack, and the smell of plastic and unidentifiable chemicals used to treat clothes permeates the space. Thick lines of tape guide one's walking path, a legal requirement to ensure fire safety in what is an ostensibly hazardous room, stuffed to the brim with goods. Sales associates regularly zoom in and out from the sales floor; customers will often demand they search in the back for their desired size—an almost always futile and sometimes dangerous endeavor. "Don't get lost in there!" a manager once playfully shouted to me as I disappeared into a double-decker rack of blouses.

Stock shifts at Style Queen began at 6 a.m. For workers commuting from New York City's outer boroughs, as most were, wake-up times could be as early as 3 or 4 a.m., especially on weekends when public transit was particularly unreliable. Based on my interviews, employees at other fast-fashion companies began their stock shifts at 3 a.m. My stockroom coworkers and I remained alienated from the workers across the supply chain: no discussion ever occurred about garment factories or warehouses from which the garments originated.[10]

Each shift, we unloaded and processes two kinds of shipments. "New pro" was new product, which was much easier to process since it was shipped to the store in larger, more organized batches. "Call offs," in contrast, were shipments to replace garments that had been recently sold. Here the "just-in-time-ness" became acutely visible, as call-off bins were completely disorganized. At the very least, the bins' contents were usually separated by major department—women's, men's, kids', and accessories—but the contents within the bins had no rhyme or reason to their order. The algorithms that dictated call offs remained invisible to us.

To process the garments, employees arranged themselves in a line on one side of a long folding table. One worker would open a bin, pull out the clothing, unfold it, and lay it out on the table. The synthetic odors were strongest here, as the scents wafted out with each opening lid and escaped the plastic bags within which more delicate items were packed. To my knowledge, no one ever complained about the smells, but I, for one was concerned: a 2012 Greenpeace report, "Toxic Threads," found that chemicals used by a number of leading retailers can be "hormone disrupting and even cancer causing."[11] The environmental consequences, the report points out, are even more pernicious in fast fashion's super-sized production cycles. Exposure to such chemicals was one of several invisible or unspoken occupational hazards.

The next staff member in line applied two-piece security tags. A sharp pin in one segment of the tag was poked through the garment and inserted into the other half of the tag. Once assembled, the pin resembled a golf ball sliced in half with a pin in the middle. Informal guidelines dictated where tags should be placed: lower left corner for shirts, under the back right belt loop for pants. The "inefficiencies of efficiency," as sociologist George Ritzer might say, were clear.[12] We regularly poked ourselves in the fingers with the pins, sometimes drawing blood. The delicate fabric of many garments would almost certainly suffer a noticeable hole when the security tag was removed. Wouldn't customers notice? Attaching a tag to one pair of socks in a multipack would leave the other pairs available for pilfering. New staff, especially, struggled to understand why we did all this. None of it made much sense, but we did what we were told, and we did it fast.

The final position in the processing assembly line was the least desirable: putting the garments on hangers and organizing them on metal rolling racks (called "ponies") according to store section, such as basics, professional, junior, swim, and trend, the latter of which may go by a special name depending on the store. Most sections have their own tag, making sorting somewhat easier. Still, attaching the hanger could be difficult and walking the garments from the table to the ponies and arranging them in the proper section required more effort than other positions on the processing line. Sorting the "call-off" inventory was especially onerous. Whoever was last in line—usually the newest employees—regularly confronted a growing backlog of clothes and a sense of never moving fast enough.

Even lacking a piece-rate system of traditional factory work (in which workers are paid based on how many items they produce or process), competition reigned. More senior employees regularly commented on the need for faster coworkers, passive-aggressively undercutting newer staff. Numerous people I interviewed admitted they tried to avoid the stockroom for precisely those reasons:

Zarina: It was a little like a sweatshop. It was kind of weird. There was an analog clock on the wall. We were standing there doing things in the line order. One person's taking all the items out of, I can't remember what they're called, the containers. Another person's hanging them, and one person's putting security sensors on them. So yeah, it was kind of weird. It was a lot physically. 'Cause you're repeating the same movements over and over.

Susanna: I didn't do it super-fast. And you had to be *super*-efficient. They had this whole system. . . . If you're not doing it in order they'll be like, "You have to do it in order, that's the fastest way to do it."

M: Did you like doing that work?

Susanna: I liked it before they told me I need to go faster, faster, faster.

I often wondered what motivated some of these low-paid, hourly workers to move so quickly. I, for one, found it exhausting. Certainly, working stock at these retail stories varied considerably from working at garment factories, but I also wondered if the stock associates might find solidarity with other workers across the supply chain.

While the work process was at its most routinized here, at the same time it felt the most free, since coworkers could spend their shifts talking to one another. Without customers to get in the way, some collective solidarity did emerge. I regularly received tips on the most efficient ways to tag garments (techniques that were more comfortable weren't always efficient, I was told), and I learned that my mothers' method of inserting a hanger from the bottom of a shirt was a big no-no. Indeed, sales assistants, scurrying to the stockroom in search of a garment, briefly relished being surrounded by peers with genuine smiles on their faces, laughing uproariously at each other's jokes.

Conversation regularly took more serious tones as well; some of my deepest interactions happened while processing clothes, usually a few hours after everyone had enough time to wake up. Life histories and the changing landscape of New York City were regularly discussed alongside music and pop culture. One morning, my coworker Christina said, "Gentrifiers want to experience the culture [of New York] but then they just steal from it." My coworker David looked at me and laughed. I was the only person in the room who hadn't grown up in New York. "It's true!" I agreed. Christina qualified: "But it's not just white people who are gentrifiers. It's companies. Like the Bronx has a Starbucks now, so you know it's over." I added, "Meanwhile we're working at Style Queen." David looked at me and raised his eyebrow in agreement: "Right?"

The stockroom similarly took on a unique character without the official store soundtrack. Sociologist Marek Korczynski describes in his ethnography of a blinds factory how music plays a central role in worker subjectivity. Music injects bodies with energy to maintain the status quo. Music can also de-alienate the work process, allowing employees to lose themselves in the music, to forget, however briefly, that their time belongs to someone else.[13] I wrote in my field notes that the beginning of the shifts on the sales floor were the worst. Time seemed to drag on forever. The only thing that saved me was hearing a song I recognized, such as a single from major pop star Taylor Swift. In any other context, I might tune the song out, but here it brought me to life. Jayla, who worked at Forever 21 in New York City, described how music marked the boundary between the sales floor and the stockroom: "the basement wasn't part of the sales floor at all . . . Once you went downstairs it turned into a completely different zone. Because people were listening to their own music or whatever.

So, it was like a nice little escape every time you got the chance to go down there."

During my summer at Style Queen, I felt haunted by Rihanna's hit song "Work." While the thrumming of Rihanna's voice helped me keep pace with my tasks on the sales floor, the repetition grated on me—both in its frequent rotation in the official store soundtrack and in its lyrics. As one music critic notes, the song "doesn't really go anywhere. It approximates what work feels like."[14] After my shift, I dreaded encountering subway passengers streaming the single from their phones. Hearing it made my heart race in Pavlovian response.

In contrast, the stockroom that summer pulsed to the sounds of Beyonce's "Sorry," which, contrary to its title, is an unapologetic tune about not being sorry, a no bosses/no boyfriends refrain. My coworkers pranced around the store wishing each other "Happy *Lemonade* Day" when Beyonce's much anticipated album dropped. *Lemonade* in many ways marked the mood not just of the stockroom but of the moment: a sense of frustration with the status quo and a Black feminist desire for new ways of being in the world. *Lemonade* likewise evinced the "cruel optimism"[15] of trying to find a way to survive while being stuck in systems of exploitation; just as Beyonce returns to her "boo" (boyfriend) at the end of the album, so too did most of us remain tethered to the employee-boss relation, as well as exploitative systems of white supremacy, capitalism, and heteropatriarchy. Possessing a soundtrack of one's own in the stockroom allowed workers to create a collective and oppositional culture, which supported, somewhat paradoxically, the survival of the workers and, by extension, the corporations that employed them. We were allowed to feel as if we had some ownership over our time, if we got our work done.

Interactive service is completely absent from this "heart of the store," the stockroom. Brands rely on customer and purchase data to determine ever-changing inventory, creating an atmosphere akin to on-demand fulfillment centers. Employees clutched to small freedoms such as soundtrack autonomy; still, the mix of unpredictability, speed, and physical strain weigh heavily. Moving away from the stockroom, the automated heart beats a little differently on the sales floor.

"A Flow of Chaos" on the Sales Floor

The critically acclaimed film *Brooklyn* (2015), set in 1952, depicts a young Irish immigrant in New York City, overcoming her intense shyness and blossoming as a department store salesperson, engaging her customers with polite, articulate conversations. The work of selling, the movie demonstrates, was part and parcel of early twentieth-century white working-class womanhood, allowing them to occupy a respectable public space and interact with sophisticated consumers.[16] Over the course of the last century, the clothing retail industry has grown to a massive scale, hugely expanding the consumer base and proletarianizing the occupation. The craft of selling, performing an intimate knowledge of the goods being sold and developing relationships with customers, might have been central to earlier iterations of retail labor—and to Hochschild's "managed heart"—but those aspects are foreign to most people working in fast fashion today.

Again, it's helpful to look at job advertisements to see what fast-fashion retailers look for in employees. The following is an ad for a sales associate position:

> We don't call them "salespeople" or "sales associates" because that's not what we do. Our Sales Advisors are here to ensure that our customers enjoy a fantastic shopping experience, whether it's offering them garment options or answering simple questions such as locating the fitting rooms. Because, in the end, we believe that our clothes will sell themselves.

Even from this advertisement, the distinctions between fast fashion and other forms of retail labor are clear. We see that selling is "not what we do" because indeed the "clothes will sell themselves." My interviewees articulated what this looks like in practice. The following is how some interviewees responded when I asked them to describe their primary tasks:

Kya: Mostly working on the floor and putting the clothes back in the section they belonged to. That was the main task I would do when I was there.

Zee: Mostly just cleaning, organizing, being efficient about getting everything done on a certain schedule; mostly, my job honestly was cleaning up after others, helping them finish their tasks.

Rachel: To me the biggest thing that was stressed was keeping the store clean. And the store did have visual standards, which I appreciated. Everything had to have, you know, they wanted the size run [ordering garments by size] and they wanted the hangers facing the same way and they wanted the face-outs [garments on the end of a rack that are visible to customers] to look a certain, you know. I remember even my first week there were a couple days I literally spent six hours folding pants. 'Cause there's like seven ways to fold pants. Which I had no idea! So I mean, I feel like that was the first goal.

One of my interviewees, Zee, articulated the overall confusion of the sales floor aptly:

> While you're on the floor, it's like swimming. 'Cause you're trying to clean up trash, and you're customer servicing at the same time. So, you get into this flow of where you walk around. So that there's a standard for, like, how you fold your shirts, how all the various fixtures and tables should look. Things sort of like, there's sort of a flow of chaos, where we know, like, oh, that table's gonna get messed up, let's keep an eye on it. Or, oh, a huge group [of customers] went into that corner, I'm gonna keep tabs on 'em. Very organized. Very organized.

In Zee's rendering, customers always come second to the primary task of keeping up a clean and orderly store. Their final few snippets—"Very organized. Very organized."—sounded to me like an attempt to verbally manifest something that remains immanently out of reach. And Kya and Rachel don't mention customers at all. Clothing retail has always included some cleaning up after the customer, but these quotes highlight the extent to which focusing on *things* supersedes any efforts to provide interactive service.

Managers instruct sales associates to spend the first few minutes of each shift simply walking around their section to get a sense of the sales floor. Since the floor layout constantly changes, workers must redevelop a situational awareness of where garments are located or what might have been moved since the last shift. Most stores are overflowing with clothing, and racks burst in an explosion of styles and colors. Rachel, who worked at Zara, told me: "[The store's] entire floor set changes every two weeks. So, one of managers, who trained me so well, she was like, 'The first thing you do when you come into this store, when you go on the floor to start working, take just like two seconds and walk the floor and just visually see what's going on.'" The remainder of the shift consists of doing "go-backs," meaning returning unwanted garments from the fitting room to their proper spot on the sales floor and putting away garments that have been processed by the stockroom, all the while dealing with (or, more often, avoiding) customers.

Rachel describes the exhaustion that can result from go-backs: "Sometimes, like, I would be doing go-backs and I would have a shirt in my hand, and I would look for it for like twenty minutes. I would look at my friend and be like, where the *hell* is this dang shirt? And he'd be like, it's right there. And I'd be like, *ohhh*, what? Just, of course it is. So, it was hard to kinda know, like, *every* single thing." I smiled as Rachel told me this because I could relate to it. I often told friends that working in fast fashion made me feel crazy: I would meander in circles around my section, determined to find a blouse I knew I had seen just moments before. I would think I saw the blouse out of the corner of my eye, for a split second enjoying the rush—ah yes, I finally found it! Soon I would discover that what I had located was not the blouse in my hand, but rather another, cruelly similar design: a *different* white frilly shirt, or a shirt of the same pattern but in a tunic rather than a crop-top style.

"Do you work here tomorrow?" one of my coworkers asked me toward the end of a particularly stressful shift. I told her I didn't, to which she replied, "Well that's good, 'cause you would get really frustrated. They're gonna change it all around tonight."

The swirl of go-backs echoes the combination of unpredictability and speed found in the stockroom. In both places, we see how the rise of an automated heart doesn't necessarily equate to twenty-first-century Taylorism. In other words, in absence of interactive service, these retail workers still are not performing the same task over and over again. They perform the same *kind* of task, but because of the constant shifts in inventory, the details of the task are always changing. Following Jeffrey Sallaz's study of call-center workers, the fast-fashion retail experience is governed less by despotic management overseeing every move in attempts to enact standard precision than by what Sallaz calls "permanent pedagogy."[17] Sallaz finds that in the call-center context, employees are given very little training, requiring consistently high effort from workers, who must navigate ever-changing customer inquiries and are provided with few long-term rewards. Of the employee turnover this work process engenders, Sallaz writes, "No matter. By now, a new batch of agents is ready to enter the queue, and the system of permanent pedagogy continues to churn."[18]

Similarly, in fast fashion, the work of maintaining the sales floor requires reorienting oneself to the inventory with every shift, never gaining full knowledge of the floor nor the products sold. Workers have no long-term incentive to keep playing the game other than desperation for menial wages or some comfort of coworker camaraderie. The constant rush of the sales-floor sorting game comes with notable mental and physical costs: I, as well as the workers with whom I spoke, regularly experienced complete exhaustion, head and body aches, and hand pain and redness from garment hangers digging into our palms.

Sallaz's discussion leaves out the everyday opportunities for subversion that permanent pedagogy creates and indeed requires. When one can never conquer the game, one can at least find shortcuts, and I found both employees and management openly acknowledged some of these tricks. For instance, workers who cannot determine the proper location of the go-back are to "blend" the garment, putting it alongside similar colors or styles to at least not appear too out of place. Although this strategy is meant to create an appearance of organization when stock runs low—a lone white, ruffled shirt doesn't look so bad if it's placed next to other white shirts—it is also a key survival tactic for the exhausted worker who simply cannot bear to wander around their section once more.

Jesse, a former Forever 21 employee, practiced similar moves. Although Forever 21 was much more fast-paced than the discount store where he previously worked, he said he had more leeway to get things done on his own terms.

Jesse: Even after six months there we still spent so much time looking at clothes, being like, is this [section a]? Is this [section b]? We're just gonna put this here [chuckles].

M: Did you ever get reprimanded for that at all?

Jesse: Let me think. No, not reprimanded for putting something in the wrong section, but I know other people were for sure. And I think that's because they would say, "Oh this is in the wrong section, who did this?" [lowers voice] I wouldn't say anything even if it was me.

. . .

M: When you were a sales associate, did you come up with tricks to get things done efficiently?

Jesse: Um [laughs], I was really good at hiding things. I was really good at reorganizing racks so they seemed less full. Condensing was also a big thing. In the men's department something that really helped me was, on the racks, building outfits. So not on mannequins but on the racks themselves, you would style something, and I was really good at just, like, really layering that.

One of the most important skills Jesse learned is how to hide his mishaps, using the abundant inventory to his own advantage. In Sallaz's case of call-center workers, permanent pedagogy arose from the unpredictability of the customer service encounter. For fast-fashion workers, the constant rotation of inventory created the primary concern and main source of unpredictability.

In contrast to Jesse, other employees simply keep up the appearance of working, like Ryan:

M: Do you ever see people slacking off while they're working?

Ryan: Of course.

M: Can you tell me how people do that? How do they get away with it?

Ryan: You know, you'll just, like, fold the same sweater over and over again.

I once again thought of the interview games at Style Queen, described in the previous chapter. I quickly learned I could never fully please the manager, so I had to merely look like I was working.

At first blush, we might imagine employees like Jesse—who feel comfortable hiding clothes rather than seeking out their proper location—or Ryan—who might fold the same garments repeatedly—as fast fashion's antagonists, refusing the demands of a sped-up, under-remunerated workplace. And yet, as with stockroom soundtracks, these subaltern forms of refusal simultaneously ensure the survival of both the worker and the employer. In fast fashion, a perfectly organized sales floor is an unattainable ideal, toward which managers push their team, but even without which the store can continue to flourish.

Customers have not completely disappeared from the equation, however. In fact, there are probably more customers than ever, zooming in and out and around the store. McFashion and Style Queen managers repeatedly told us that our employment deeply relied on customers—one claimed to respond to customers by saying, "No, *thank you*—without you I wouldn't have a job!" Yet on the sales floor, customers often felt more like a distraction from, if not a direct threat to, the task of maintaining the order of the floor.

A few workers I interviewed told me they were trained to refrain from providing too much customer service. Zee said, "For instance, I was being kinda weird at first, in the beginning saying hello to everyone, and a couple coworkers found that annoying. So, they pulled me aside and were, like, you need to sort of chill out." Zee discovered "being weird" meant actively approaching every customer. Elijah similarly became visibly frustrated during our interview, raising his voice as he explained his desire to help out at the cash register when the lines grew long: "[Managers] had certain people they would send for help. They would say, beyond that, we can't spare anybody else. Which was a lie. I would say, screw that!" From the perspective of the manager, prioritizing the customer in this case distracts from the work of keeping the floor in order. While Elijah disagreed with this approach, there is some truth to it: ignoring the floor for even a few minutes could lead to frustrating messes and a backlog of clothes to be put away. At nonunionized stores, evening shift employees endure the consequences of this backlog, staying several hours after closing to put all the garments in their proper place.

Zee's and Elijah's urges to interact with customers was somewhat rare among interviewees and differed from my own experience. Associates commonly felt that shoppers got in the way of work, either asking questions that took away from the worker's current task or messing up the clothes they just organized. I learned a cruel lesson, which I documented early on in my McFashion field notes:

> In another instance in the girls' section, a group of four or five girls, maybe around 12 years old, walked around

> the department. "This is *so cute!*" they exclaimed to each other. One of the girls knocked over a pile of denim shorts and walked away. I made eye contact with her friend, and though I managed to prevent myself from glaring, I must have looked at her sternly enough, because she picked up the shorts and put them back as best as she could.

Zarina, who worked at Forever 21 in Canada, said:

> When I first started, I wanted to do things the right way and wanted to take my time. Make sure everything was organized, neat, folded properly. Then realizing it was a fast fashion store. So, people would see you folding and, like, come and knock the entire table over. [M laughs] And you're just like, What the hell? I just spent fifteen minutes doing that. So, after a while I just learned that as long as it looked presentable and nothing was on the floor, it was fine.

In this context of customer as the enemy of order, worker shortcuts again became key. A manager might reprimand a worker if an entire table looks messy, so rather than folding every shirt—which shoppers tear apart in matter of seconds—the employee might instead fold only the top few shirts to provide superficial organization.

According to customers' online testimonies, workers' pressures to put things in their proper location as quickly as possible creates dangers for shoppers as well. One customer remarked: "Was all-but-bodychecked by people working the floor while I shopped. No one helped me reach an item that was high up, despite the fact that I was obviously trying for several minutes." Another warned: "An angry little salesperson almost hit me with a clothing rack. Beware if you're pregnant."

While I never experienced or witnessed staff attempting to harm customers as the above commenters claim, the following comment felt incredibly familiar:

> I walked around for 30 minutes trying to find a specific shirt. I decided to ask someone for help they sent me to the lower floor, walked around even more. Asked someone else, he wanted to send me back upstairs. He then told me to look in their 90s section, I couldn't tell where that section was supposed to be. So again, ask someone else, he points to the back and says it should be there. Well, I had already looked and nothing. I even had pulled up a picture to show them all. After the third person being very useless and not even bothering to help me look or at least navigate me to the correct section, I gave up and left without the shirt. I wasn't even asking for them to search for it, just decent guidance.

Here, as modeled in the group interviews of the previous chapter, the customer is merely a distraction from the real work, like a ball to be juggled and passed on to the next employee.

If I prepared any rote lines to say to customers, it was usually something like, "Sorry, I don't know where that is." An automated heart, coupled with global just-in-time supply chain, allows fast fashion to provide customers with more clothing options than ever before.

As a result, it's nearly impossible to imagine a human employee being able to offer much help to customers, even if they want to.

"Garment Caring" in the Fitting Room

One might expect much more direct customer interaction in the fitting room. Yet, even here, the work of the fast-fashion fitting-room attendant has been largely reduced to logistics: regulating the number of customers coming in and the number of items they try on, taking their unwanted garments, and preparing items to be restocked on the sales floor.

Fitting rooms are colloquially known as an easy place to steal. Fitting-room attendants thus often began each shift by making their rounds to each dressing room, gliding their hands behind the mirror and collecting tags hidden by shoplifters. At one of our first shifts, my coworker, also a newbie, took a spin, returning with a smile on her face as her hands overflowed with tags. McFashion was somehow kind enough to assign two workers per fitting room shift—allowing one employee to escort guests to the fitting rooms while the other sorted garments and prepared them to return to the floor.

I got used to this help at McFashion and suffered for it at Style Queen—David, my mentor during the first few weeks, burst out laughing when I asked him if I would have another person helping me out. I was soon overwhelmed with the deluge of customers, and as usual, standards remained virtually impossible to reach, especially during high-traffic periods. Customers approached the fitting room, we counted their items (only seven maximum allowed), escorted them individually to an available room, placed their garments inside, and hung their item number outside each room. I quickly became physically exhausted walking back and forth. If customers had more than seven items, we hung the extras on a pony near the front of the fitting area. It wasn't uncommon for those items to disappear or make their way back to the sales floor before the customer returned to claim them.

One woman I interviewed, Kya, who was in New York on a film internship, had worked at a Forever 21 in Ohio. She told me about a few especially tense moments after she accidentally returned a customer's garments to the sales floor: "I remember [the customer] was yelling because her stuff was like [gone], and there's no process for like, who knows where it could be, in the whole store." Kya added sarcastically, "[Customers] got very upset about their Forever 21 clothes." We both laughed at the absurdity of the shoppers caring about such poorly made goods, and their naiveté about the social contract of fast fashion, in which good customer service is rarely part of the equation. Negative online reviews of fitting-room attendants flourish, while others read like warnings:

> Staff is always tidying up the floor/fitting room so maybe that's why they're not so pleasant (they seemed fine to me).
>
> Normally there is zero service at [these stores] and the associates in the changing rooms are just futz-ing around.
>
> I've had fine service here. It's [fast fashion], I'm not expecting anything amazing but it's been good.
>
> While I was there, the dressing rooms were pretty crowded. . . . The workers there are also have that "I really don't care" attitude, but who can blame them? It's retail and they probably have to deal with more tourists than Ellis Island.

These reviews in some ways reflect the growing pains customers go through as they must relearn the price they pay for such cheap goods; some customers appear angry. Others ask, "What do you expect?"

Off the internet and away from keyboard, workers shoulder the consequences of these growing pains.[19] During one particularly busy shift, as I raced up and down the fitting room walkway, a petite, elderly woman peeled back her fitting room curtain, peered her head out, and asked politely, "Can you find this in a small?" I replied with a sigh, "I'm so sorry, I can't leave the fitting room right now." Store policy dictated that an attendant should always remain in the fitting room while customers were inside, though attendants made exceptions during periods of unusually slow traffic (a more common occurrence in the men's section).

Sociologist Lynne Pettinger argues that retail employees do the work of making self-service possible: "Workers' ability to give personal services to the few who demand them is posited on sales organised so that the majority of customers serve themselves."[20] The role of the fitting-room attendant is no longer to attend to every person trying on clothes, but to make sure rooms are available and clean so that a customer can attend to themself.

Although we instructed customers to return unwanted garments to us, we more often collected mountains of unwanted clothes from the fitting rooms. These wads of inside-out, unbuttoned, unzipped clothes subsequently had to be "garment cared," or made presentable for the sales floor, before being hung on the pony in the correct section. The term "garment care" is significant here. We are caring not for the customer but for the garment. A manager making her rounds in the fitting room once muttered, "Nobody garment cares" as she buttoned a blouse. Equally significant, never did she, nor any other manager, reprimand me for poor customer service.

Multiple workers I interviewed told me they were never assessed on their customer service skills because their stores were such "cash cows." Rachel, who had worked at Zara in Los Angeles, told me:

> I didn't have to worry about [sales]. That's what I liked [about] working there. It was a cash cow, and we didn't have to worry, we were always gonna go over our goal. It was easy and I didn't have the pressure of

> most places. 'Cause I worked at Saks [Fifth Avenue] for a while after and we had commission. You know it's such a pain in your back. It was sales, sales, sales. And at Zara, nobody really cared because we knew we were gonna go over our goal anyway.

Similarly, Jayla had worked in fast fashion several years ago. She told me her store used secret shoppers, who would roam the floors disguised as shoppers, rating their experience and interactions. Jayla told me that even when they received low scores, not much happened. "They were pretty lenient about it. The store was such a cash cow that, like, they weren't gonna close us down or anything, whatever. . . . It was the kind of thing like I said we had a fitting room with clothing to the fucking ceiling. Sorry [for cursing]."

Significantly, the fitting room served as a site of escape for sales associates and shoppers alike, one of the few areas throughout the store removed from the panoptic gaze. If stockrooms were the heart of the store, the fitting rooms were the release valve. There was no closed-circuit television and relatively little human oversight, except for the managers sporadically popping in and out. Filipe, a muscular sales attendant, regularly absconded to the fitting room, pulling his cell phone out of his khaki pants pocket as he looked at himself in the mirror. "What are you doing back there?" some coworkers jokingly shouted. "I'm sending a text! What do you think?" Filipe shouted back, like an annoyed sibling. Filipe had no regard for clientele who might notice his behavior. Susanna, a former H&M employee, once rushed to the fitting room to cry after a distressing encounter with a homophobic customer.

Fitting-room attendants likewise had more leeway than the more actively monitored sales associates. Throughout one afternoon shift on the sales floor, I fetched go-backs from the fitting room attended by Dana, a middle-aged woman and one of the few full-time Style Queen employees. Dana regularly refused the imperative to rush, rarely performed "garment care," and often sent items back to the wrong sections. "This is completely against store regulation, but I don't care," she said as she slowly wrapped a silk robe around her torso and admired her full-length reflection. "I look good in this." During a busier part of the shift, a gaggle of customers rushed at Dana with armfuls of unwanted clothes. "I only have two hands," she sternly reminded them. Later, I watched a customer emerge from the fitting room and hold out her garments with her arms extended, looking at no one in particular. "I'm over here!" Dana shouted. "We're invisible to them," she muttered when the customer walked away. Sociologist C. Wright Mills might have called Dana an "old-timer," who "is against [store] policies . . . and often she turns her sarcasm and rancor upon the customer."[21] I admired Dana's demeanor, and the shadows of the fitting room allowed her space and freedom to demand dignity and respect.

The fitting room occasionally offered a means of escape for customers as well because it was one of the few places where shoppers could sit down inside the store. Exhausted patrons regularly took a moment's rest on tables on the sales floor, but this was explicitly against store policy. More than once, I went to the front office to find a manager, only to be asked by the loss prevention specialist, who scanned security cameras from behind a closed door, to get shoppers off the tables. In the fitting room, people quickly snatched the chairs near the back, and on more than one occasion I encountered worn-out shoppers resting their eyes while slouched on a small bench tucked away in the corner. I made a conscious effort not to disturb them there. In those fleeting moments, I hoped this space of consumption and exploitation could also serve as a site of refuge—recalling what surveillance scholar Simone Browne calls "the productive processes of being unseen"[22]–a hideaway for all those not willing or able to incessantly work or shop.

Garment rooms in the era of the automated heart are not officially devoid of care. But here again, staff are told to direct their care first to commodities—the garments—not the customers. An automated heart more efficiently taps into consumer desires, replenishing stores with an endless stream of things to buy, but also results in fitting rooms piled "to the fucking ceiling" of unwanted clothing.

These tensions between the scale and speed of an automated heart and the limits of human labor became even more pronounced at the cash register.

Cash Register Queues

If a customer survives their trip through the store, makes it through the wait at the fitting room, and ultimately decides to make a purchase, the cash register presents the final challenge, the last hurdle standing between them and their new outfit. The price and quality of the commodity in these cases can swing the customer in two directions: they may either decide that the bargain is worth enduring the long lines or (as I have admittedly done) second-guess the entire pursuit, realizing they do not in fact *need* this garment badly enough to wait in line. The cash register thus serves as a choke point in the fast-fashion transaction, where the friction between customers and employees often comes to a head.

Because of this pressure, cashiers take on one of the most stressful roles in the store, in which customers expect speed, accuracy, and some semblance of politeness. I was, much to my relief, rarely assigned to work at the register, but training for the role proved stressful enough. At the beginning of each shift, the McFashion register needed to start at $200 and not one penny off. I attempted to count my register and had to repeat the process three or four times: the first time I forgot to include the rolls of change stored underneath the drawer, and the other times I simply miscounted. "What's taking everyone so long?" asked our manager, Stacey, with annoyance. Thankfully, others struggled alongside me. As I watched one of the trainers count the drawer for one of the other trainees, I noticed he utilized a specific method of counting change by putting half of the pennies in each hand and then quickly dropping them in alternating intervals. I was reminded that all these tasks were in fact acquired skills. Adding to my anxiety, the McFashion return policy says customers may only receive store credit for returns. This policy even applied to cases of employee error; hypothetically, if a cashier charged a customer twice, and the customer didn't notice or speak up until the transaction was complete, the customer would be eligible for a gift card in the amount of the erroneous charge, but could not receive cash or money back on their credit card. "All because the cashier wasn't paying attention," Stacey warned us. This scenario represents yet another negative externality carried by low-wage workers, a downfall of the fast-fashion model framed as worker inefficiency.

My cashier training at Style Queen didn't go much better. I expressed my nervousness to my coworker, who said to me, "You're young, you've used a cash register before, right? You'll be fine." Little did she know I was in fact nearly ten years her senior and hadn't used a register in at least fifteen years. My trainer, Sofia—a short woman with dark eyeliner and dirty fingernails (which I appreciated in this world so obsessed with aesthetics)—brought with her a packet that said the training should last two hours. Sofia breezed through, reading directly from the packet and often skipping entire sections. We talked about how to ring up purchases, the importance of making sure each item scans, the order in which items are rung up (scan them, take the hangers off, take the sensors off, fold them, and then put them in the bag), how to correct mistakes, and the distinction between different forms of payment. Sofia clarified applying discounts to single items versus the whole purchase—if it's buy-two-get-one-free, then all the items must be grouped together when we ring them up. We also talked about how to ring up a gift card and how to perform returns or exchanges. To do an exchange one must do a complete return, put the amount on the gift card, and then ring up the item they want to purchase with the gift card. If the item doesn't have a price tag, we have to look it up by the number on the garment tag. To do a return we have to check the receipt, make sure the purchase occurred within the last thirty days, make sure they are returning the proper item, scan the receipt, select the proper item on the computer, then redeem the money on the original form of payment. If a person making a return doesn't have their ID, or if it's not within thirty days of the purchase, they only get store credit.

Not only was this a huge amount of information to retain, but the surrounding environment significantly added to the chaos—Sofia herself became visibly flustered. How could one not? The register beeped when the security tags were too close to the tag remover, and sometimes both our register and the one next to us would beep loudly at different intervals. Meanwhile, the music blared so loudly that at certain moments, I truly could not hear myself think. Another worker approached Sofia and asked her when her shift was over. Sofia replied, "I'm supposed to be gone already but I gotta finish this training!" "Oh no, I'm so sorry!" I apologized. "It's fine, I knew this would take a while." Meanwhile, customers approached the counter, expecting Sofia to help them; Sofia just refused to make eye contact and avoided their glares, a classic strategy.

My interviewees and coworkers likewise often found that working the cash register was anxiety-inducing. One coworker who looked cool as a cucumber from a distance raced from the register over to me on the sales floor. "Do you know how to do gift cards?" he frantically asked, beads of sweat forming on his forehead. I didn't know, so I sent him to one of our more senior coworkers around the corner. My interviewees shared similar stories:

Zarina: It took me awhile to get cash-trained after getting hired there. It was a little more stressful because the lineups would be constant. Especially during the holidays or when we would have collaborations with designers. It would just be a lot to keep going. Deal with one customer, they make a $300 purchase, then deal with another customer. Also diffusing situations when things come up. That's supposed to be on sale but it's not on sale. Having to contact someone on the floor to look up the price or confirm the price. So that was a little stressful.

Kya: And they tried to train me on it [the register] but it was just bad. Somebody gave me $100. I dunno if I didn't realize it, or I put it in the thing wrong, but I gave them the incorrect change back. And so, they were very [upset], and the person [supervisor] had to come in. So, at the end of the day, when I was done, my till was all the way off. The first time I did it, it was way off, and the second time I did it, it was less. But they were just like, okay, we're just not gonna have you there.

Rachel: Yeah, it was crazy. . . . I had never been on a register before. There's lines down and around the corner. People usually buy like a hundred things at once. So, check the credit card, check the IDs, take the sensor off, you know, talk to them; also, like, it was just like counting the register. All of this, it was like, and I am not good at math. I went to a fashion school for Christ's sake. It was a lot of pressure and it just made me really anxious. So, after my training, I simply told my manager, I don't wanna do that. It's too much.

Although Rachel successfully refused the cashier role, in my fieldwork, employees had little autonomy over where they would be assigned to work that day. Part of the stress of the cash register stemmed from the tension that workers could never perform as quickly as the customer desired. When a customer returned something, we had to "garment care" it, or make sure it was ready to be properly restocked on the sales floor, which meant turning our backs to the growing lines so we could zip zippers and button buttons. To a customer, this behavior may appear tangential to the cashier role. We might look like we are flat-out ignoring the customer. And while managers at McFashion sometimes told us it was okay to jump on a register for a few minutes if we noticed lines getting long, doing so would put our work on the sales floor at risk of coming completely undone.

In reviewing online customer comments about cashiers, I found that criticisms revolved around three themes. First is the abundance of sales associates but lack of cashiers. "There were five employees walking around aimlessly looking at us like we're dumb while we're in line waiting with no one providing the only cashier with help." Comments in this vein indicate the extent to which shoppers remain largely unaware of the material labor required to keep the store running.

The second theme of complaints focuses on cashier speed, or lack thereof. "The cashiers are slower than a snail unaware that you have places to go, clothes to put on." "It's highly unpleasant shopping here. I'm always with a baby and we literally wait thirty minutes in line to pay for just a couple of items." These reviewers imply the slow workers are subhuman, but I wonder if anything other than a super-human could keep up. In addition, these reviewers invoke a long-running tradition of rebuking workers, especially Black workers, for being slow, for dragging their feet, or enacting any subtle form of resistance against either the boss or the customer.[23]

Finally, the third source of customer frustration centered on the lack of customer service:

> There ought to be a zero-star rating to properly rate this place! I get better service in a South Bronx bodega. . . . I asked [the manager] if he ever said thank you to customers (after watching him dispassionately ring up the five women in front of me without a single hello, bit of eye contact or a thank you) and he said no. Wow! It's true.

> Unfortunately, it's *always* a miserable experience when you get to check out. Most of the time there's only two people working at checkout and they are beyond slow. Every time I've been [there] the person cashing me out is chatting away with fellow coworkers. Not just chatting but complaining about how much their life sucks for having this job. Save it for later when customers aren't around.

In some ways, with the rise of online review sites, customers have seemingly replaced mystery shoppers, with the power to document any negative interaction for all to see. And yet service without a smile matters little when clothes sell themselves. What does matter—and where these snags in the system reveal potential holes—is when automation turbocharges many aspects of the retail process, while expecting its human staff to keep pace.

Sociological Implications of the Automated Heart

Like other iterations of retail, whether department store, branded apparel, or big box retailing, fast fashion attempts to manage a series of pressures endemic to the labor process: store upkeep, incentivizing employees to constantly accelerate their work pace, creating a veneer of workplace community, while suppressing collective worker struggle. If Susan Porter-Benson describes department stores as a product of "mass consumption," then fast fashion is a product of 24/7 capitalism and constant, on-demand consumption.[24] In the drive to offer shoppers an incessant stream of trendy, low-priced goods, retail companies rely on big data to track consumer preferences and desires, and frontline labor must prioritize the quickening shuffle of commodities in and through the store.

The shift away from customer service in the retail setting—from a managed heart to an automated heart—has numerous implications for sociologists, labor activists, and anyone concerned about the changing nature of work in the twenty-first century. First, this shift challenges how researchers conceptualize service work, moving away from the dominant frameworks of interactive labor. The jobs people refer to when they say "service work" might not actually include a lot of worker-customer contact.

In this chapter we've seen how by digitizing knowledge of consumer desire, fast-fashion retail labor has been deskilled and sped up, and workers have been made disposable. They might be "controlled in more impersonal ways" as Hochschild suggests, but this has not made the work any easier. In fact, workers seem to be pushed to ever further extremes, and the physical demand of working in fast fashion wears out the workers almost as quickly as the clothing being sold wears out. As we'll see in the next chapter, automation of customer service has emerged alongside the rise of digital worker surveillance.

4
How Retailers Use New Technologies to Surveil Workers

"I think she was just trying to scare us," my coworker Ana told me.[1] We had completed our new employee orientation at McFashion and were waiting in line to scan our fingerprints, so they'd be on file with the company bioscanner. The last time I remembered someone keeping my fingerprints on file was when I was arrested for public intoxication in college. However, we were assured the bioscanner was both accurate and convenient. No need to worry about what time it was; the bioscanner kept track of that for us. I had told Ana I thought it was strange that we were assured that working at McFashion would be easy and fun, but we were also warned that someone was always watching us even if we didn't realize it. Ana shrugged. She didn't seem too concerned, but I couldn't quite make sense of this combination of playfulness and creepiness.

The orientation had begun two hours earlier when I found myself sitting with forty or so other new hires at the back of the store. I was excited to finally start working after waiting over a month since being hired to get called back, in part because I was feeling strapped for cash. I tried to pay attention to the training manager, Jo, a petite twenty-one-year-old who had been with the company for nine months. I admittedly had a hard time concentrating. The store soundtrack was bumping as usual, and I shivered from the arctic-blast air conditioning. My back ached from the stiff, metal folding chair and reminded me that I was indeed older than most of my new coworkers. "This is literally the most people I've ever trained before," Jo said, "so I'm gonna have to be yelling at you."

Over the course of our two-hour review of the employee handbook, Jo explained many things, including the elaborate procedure we were to follow when coming and going from the store. Before we clocked in on the first floor, we were to secure our belongings in an employee locker on the third floor. Then we returned to the first floor where the bioscanner was located at the end of a long line of cash registers. Clocking in even just one minute late was considered tardy, but we also were not allowed to clock in more than five minutes prior to the beginning of our shift. Before we clocked out, we were to have our bags checked by security to make sure we hadn't stolen any merchandise.

The handbook also stated that anything we posted on social media could potentially be accessed by McFashion. Jo warned us about one employee who was working in the fitting room and had apparently posted a selfie on Instagram with the caption: "Supposed to be working. Haha

#timestealing." I tried to keep my mouth from hanging open. I was shocked and, to be honest, impressed. Even though the employee quickly realized her error and deleted her post, Jo assured us that a manager who followed this employee online had taken a screenshot of her post and appropriately disciplined her. On another occasion, an employee said he couldn't come in because his mother was in the hospital. Later that evening, he posted pictures online "popping bottles in the club." The moral of these stories? Employee tracking went well beyond the physical confines of the store. Even in cyberspace, our behavior could be seen and punished.

Despite throwing all these rules at us, Jo regularly peppered the training with jokes and tips about how to evade trouble. We weren't supposed to stand around chatting with friends who visited the store. Jo suggested, "Just walk and talk. You'll be less likely to get caught that way." On the topic of alcohol and drug abuse, she said, "I'm sure you all drink, even if you're not twenty-one years old yet. And trust me you'll need a shot after your shift! Just make sure you do it on your own time." *Perhaps this was all part of the plan,* I wrote in my field notes that evening, *always blurring the line between boss and friend, work and fun.*

My McFashion orientation clued me in to how retailers are concerned with cataloging and thwarting various kinds of "shrink," or lost revenue. The most well-known is what retailers call "external theft" by shoppers or organized crime rings. As I was coming to learn, retailers also anticipate "internal" shrink by employees. Clearly, this was where the employee bag checks came in. Digital tools prevented additional forms of internal shrinkage, such as "time stealing," when employees are paid for time not worked. It could be as little as a few minutes but supposedly added up to big costs for corporations. That explained why McFashion was such a stickler about clocking in with the bioscanner and warned us about posting on social media while on the clock. According to a 2020 survey by the National Retail Federation, "dishonest employee" cases—including theft, time stealing, or "sweethearting" (when workers give their friends special discounts)—cost retailers an average of $1,139.32 per case.[2]

Social theorist Bernard Harcourt helps makes sense of how working at McFashion was framed as fun even while its employees were treated like potential criminals. Harcourt says the mix of desire and discipline is central to life in the digital age. What's unique to this "expository society," as he calls it, is that people are disciplined not just with authoritarian, top-down forms of punishment. In addition, people willingly engage in activities—like social media—that simultaneously entertain and surveil through exposing our thoughts, feelings, and behaviors: "so many of us are giving all our most intimate information and whereabouts so willingly and passionately—so voluntarily."[3]

Consider the employee who posted the #timestealing selfie. That post might have offered temporary reprieve from a boring shift, luring her in with the potential dopamine hit of racking up likes and comments. But the post also told her manager exactly what she was doing—not working when she should be—and led to her punishment and perhaps even termination. Managers like Jo sure seemed friendly; why *wouldn't* we want them to follow us online? That blurring of connection and coercion makes the potential boundaries of surveillance almost limitless.

In the last chapter, we saw how the automated heart impacted the labor process, speeding up work, removing customer service, and causing employees stress and anxiety. Here, I began to see how digitization impacted another piece of the puzzle: widespread surveillance, made possible by an array of digital tools, masqueraded as convenience and entertainment, allowing retailers to build trust with workers while tracking them in new ways. In the early twentieth century, employers hired spies from the Pinkerton National Detective Agency to monitor worker behavior and prevent labor organizing. As Harcourt says, and as my new employee orientation began to reveal, today there's little need for such dramatic human intervention. In the twenty-first century, employers leverage the help of *digital pinkertons* to keep workers in line.

NRF Protect

Fast forward to June 2016. I boarded a bus to Philadelphia for the nation's largest annual retail "loss prevention" conference, NRF Protect, hosted by the National Retail Federation (NRF). This sector of the retail industry attempts to prevent any form of shrinkage. Beyond what I had already become privy to as an employee, I wanted to "study up," to know more about how the latest digital security products were marketed and sold to retailers. It wasn't difficult for me to get into the conference. I registered as a student and was candid with everyone I spoke to about my research on retail worker surveillance. Just as my whiteness helped me stand out among retail applicants, here it helped me fit in.

I donned my most conservative business casual attire, and when I arrived at the convention center, I was greeted with thumping pop music—a soundtrack similar to what I had been subjected to for months on end as a fast-fashion employee. Vendors drew in conference goers with games and contests, and, here again, discipline was mixed with pleasure. I nabbed a free jump drive and organic lip balm emblazoned with the logo of a fraud detection service, played mini-golf, and even entered a contest to win a personal drone. Near the front of the exhibit hall, I encountered one of the more perverse setups, offering passersby staged mug shots, complete with a faux lineup backdrop and props like mustaches and cowboy hats.

In essence, the conference was a festival of the retail criminal, obsessed with detecting and sorting out bad seeds, rogue shoplifters, and insurgent time stealers.

Throughout the exhibit hall, I saw how the loss prevention industry capitalized on digitization and automation, hyping the ease with which retailers could cut costs and catch "criminals." Between breakout sessions about prescriptive analytics, social media monitoring, and exception-based reporting (more on that later), representatives from over a hundred loss prevention companies hawked their latest systems that tracked both customer and employee behavior alike.

The longer I remained at the conference, the more overt the connection between optimizing labor and policing became. One vendor I spoke to told me about how their company created a database in which members (which currently consisted of around sixty major retailers) would enter information regarding employee theft or dishonesty. Then, retailers hiring new employees could run their background checks through this database. As the vendor told me: "The way we set it up is, you have to be a member of the association, and you have to provide the data. And we then just house it and maintain it."

This database relates to one of the major concerns about big data, which is how information travels across different contexts.[4] Prior to the invention of this database, workers accused of theft might be able to get hired at a different company with a relatively clean slate if they hadn't been charged with a crime. And even if they had been charged, "ban the box" laws in many states prevent employers from including questions about criminal history on applications. These digital information warehouses bypass those laws, allowing workers' pasts to haunt them and impact their future life chances. As Ruha Benjamin writes, "'Data sharing,' for instance, sounds like a positive development so the public can access goods and services faster. But access goes both ways. If someone is marked 'risky' in one arena, that stigma follows him around much more efficiently, streamlining marginalization."[5] In other words, supposedly objective tools, such as this retailer database, can further entrench inequality.

I also encountered several facial recognition products, which have grown increasingly common in retail settings.[6] One advertisement I saw read: "While the main markets for face recognition technology remain identity management and physical security, use cases now also include commercial/service-based applications for business operations and personal use." This brochure was just one of many that revealed how much of the technology on which the retail industry now relies was in fact pioneered for law enforcement and the military. With increasing "use cases," scholars, policy makers, and others should be attuned to potential consequences.

I asked one vendor if people inside the retail stores consent to the use of facial recognition. "Well, I hope so," he responded. "We just provide the technology. We can't control what people do with it."

Think about what this might mean for workers of color. Research shows that facial recognition technology leads to disproportionately higher false positives for darker-skinned people.[7] There have been many cases where people of color have been wrongly apprehended because of being improperly identified by facial recognition software. However, few regulations govern its use. It's not a great leap to think that people who work at retailers equipped with facial recognition might be more likely to be targeted by police or other government agencies. As with the retailer database, different corporations or organizations that use the same products could very well share information among themselves.

Still, I witnessed even more overt connections between retail and police. During one breakout session, two white representatives from a St. Louis–based shoe retailer described how they survived the uprisings in Ferguson, Missouri, following the 2014 police murder of Michael Brown. They implored the audience to "take your local police chief out for lunch. It could be the best thing you do." The center of the conference hall even featured a "fusion center" where retailers could meet and build relationships with representatives from over twenty city and federal law enforcement agencies.

Surely, retail and police have always worked hand in hand. Social theorist Guy Debord once said, "What is the policeman? He is commodity's active servant."[8] But as this conference made clear, digital workplace monitoring technology facilitates that relationship and makes waged labor even more tenuous, more seamlessly subjecting low-wage employees to surveillance, reprimand, firing, or even arrest. And on top of that, many of these digital and analog connections were marketed through frameworks of ease, efficiency, and fun.

In the remainder of this chapter, I return to my ethnography on the sales floor, where I explore how automated flexible scheduling, which creates a just-in-time workforce, helps explain this rise in the "suspect flexible worker" who cannot be tracked through analog means alone.

In Touch and On Time: Biometric Fingerprint Scanners as Time Management

As I discussed in earlier in the book, automated schedulers reshape worker hours. They also lead to new modes of accounting for time worked.

At both McFashion and Style Queen, I was required to scan my fingerprint to clock in and out for shifts and lunch breaks. Biometric technology has become common across social landscapes, including prisons, welfare offices, and national borders. Because it is now required in the low-wage workplace, workers are cast as immanent threats to retailers, potential "time thieves" who can be tracked and potentially caught by new technology. Figure 4.1 features an advertisement for Kronos's

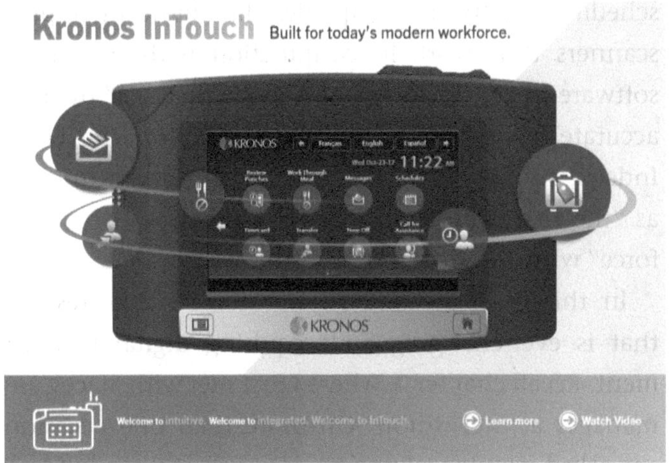

Figure 4.1
Kronos biometric scanner advertisement. *Source:* Kronos.com.

biometric scanner. Scrolling down the webpage, one would read that "with biometric identification capabilities, 'buddy punching' can be prevented to help control labor costs associated with inflated payroll." Further, "Kronos InTouch is smart enough to know whether an employee is logging in or logging out, preventing unapproved time before or after scheduled shifts and potentially inaccurate punch records. Integration also means employees can view and confirm their timecards in real time. And with the Department of Labor's increased scrutiny of hourly employee records, InTouch becomes an important tool for recording employee time and defending against potential class-action lawsuits." Recall that Kronos is one of the leading automated scheduling software companies. Biometric fingerprint scanners thus work in conjunction with scheduling software to cut down any "unnecessary costs" by more accurately accounting for time on or off the clock. Indeed, Kronos bills biometric fingerprint technology as "the first timeclock built for today's modern workforce" with "rock solid reliability."[9]

In this case, a "modern workforce" indicates one that is ever-changing and requiring digital management. Recall chapter 2, where I first met with Stacey, my manager at McFashion. On more than one occasion, she asked people walking by, "Do you still work here?" Workers were coming and going almost as frequently as shoppers, and turnover was common. So, it's no wonder managers need extra help keeping track.

But there are downsides to fingerprint scanners. Despite its supposed "rock solid" reliability, biometric technology regularly malfunctions.[10] During one of my first shifts at Style Queen, my manager, Emily, and I encountered numerous difficulties trying to register my information in the scanning system. Two biometric scanners hung on a wall in between the seating area and the staff lockers in the break room. After my manager punched a few buttons, the machine instructed me to place my finger on the scanning pad. "No finger detected," the machine read. "Try again," Emily told me, wiping the pad with a tissue. Still no finger was detected. "Maybe try a different finger," she advised. This time I used a different finger, but still, none was detected. "Let's try this machine," she said, entering her employee ID number and scanning her own finger on the machine next to us. I placed my finger on the second machine, attempting to apply more pressure, to no avail. "Put, like, your whole finger on there," she said. Alas, still no finger was detected. "Go wash your hands," she said, annoyed but not overtly frustrated, as if she had encountered similar difficulties before. I scanned my finger once more after thoroughly washing my hands. The machine then displayed the following message: "Error, no employee scheduled." To my confusion, but also relief, Emily told me, "Okay that actually means it worked. You're in the system now. But since your schedule hasn't yet been put in, it says that error. But it does log when you clock in and out, so just do that like usual and we'll be able to pay you that way."

After all that trouble, the error was apparently derived from my own sweat-induced anxiety. I trusted that the machine was properly counting my hours all that week, even as it loudly beeped each time I clocked in or out. In addition to these seemingly mundane snafus, biometric fingerprint scanners are also prone to "demographic failures," regularly failing to scan prints of elderly people, Asian women, people who work in manual or clerical industries, or people whose fingers are too large.[11]

At McFashion, the scanners malfunctioned weekly. Workers waited in long lines at shift change, hastily scrawling their hours in a notebook by pen or pencil. We hoped managers would input our time correctly, if at all. My interviewees shared similar experiences. One said, "I remember a lot of times [the scanner] didn't work. Sometimes it didn't, sometimes it did. So you'd have to put it in manually." I also had the following exchange with Susanna, who had worked at multiple fast-fashion locations along the East Coast.

Susanna: It was annoying, sometimes [the fingerprint scanner] didn't work.

M: What would you have to do when it didn't work?

Susanna: You'd have to let a manager know, and then they'd put in the time for you. And that was really annoying because, like, everything's really hectic, everything's really busy. You'd have to, like, hound them for it.

M: Did that ever happen to you?

Susanna: Yeah, a lot of times. When I first started working there, I didn't get paid for, like, weeks of work.

In these examples, the ease and efficiency of biometric scanners almost exclusively operated in employers' interests. The scanners didn't feel especially easy or efficient for workers. Instead, they amplified worker anxiety and made us prone to wage theft.

Yet, like almost all technologies, biometric scanners remained vulnerable to worker sabotage. Jesse shared: "It was hard to have someone sign in and out for you. But I know we would definitely [tell each other], just don't sign in, just say the system was down and just put your time on the paper. We'd do that for each other every now and then. Especially when we were late or things like that." Another sales associate, Vanessa, told me management at her store had become stricter about where people could clock in "because they don't want people to steal hours." When I asked if many people did that, she laughed and said yes: "I was one of them." While some might categorize Vanessa and her coworkers' behavior as deviant, she articulated it as a collective response to the stresses of automated flexible scheduling, in which algorithms calculated the optimal staffing needs, rarely with workers' needs in mind, and often with very short notice (for more on flexible scheduling, see chapter 1). She said, "They were sending us home early because they didn't have enough work [for us] to do. . . . So it was like . . . if anything, we just clock in, not clock out for thirty minutes." Not only would she partake in minor subversion, such as going to the bathroom before clocking out, but she and her coworkers began arriving as much as half an hour early, clocking in and then hanging out in the break room.

Beyond that, in my observations, employees regularly engaged in small attempts to take back time for themselves, for instance, as I mentioned in the previous chapter, by absconding to the fitting room—one of the few spaces free from CCTV's threatening gaze—to send texts, take selfies, or simply admire themselves in the mirror. Compared to the masculinist interventions that sociologist Karen Levy notes in her study of truck drivers, who would go so far as to smash their in-truck performance monitors,[12] I encountered less overt tactics of resistance to digital surveillance. My coworkers didn't take a hammer to bioscanners or surveillance cameras. They relied not on physical strength but on slyness and cunning to create a repertoire of evasion.

The discussion of *time theft* as a form of worker resistance goes alongside *wage theft*, which occurs when employees are not paid for time worked. Demos, a "think and do tank," found that more money is lost to wage theft than to shoplifting: "By paying less than the legal minimum wage, employers steal an estimated $15 billion every year. This compares to an estimated $14.7 billion lost annually to shoplifting."[13] By 2016, when I worked at Style Queen, New York State had passed an incremental wage hike, which would eventually increase wages to $15 per hour for large employers by 2018.[14] Few of my coworkers were even aware of the increase, and it's quite possible that retailers, especially nonunionized ones, were negligent in enforcing these hikes.

A form of wage theft closer to my coworkers' minds might have been how Style Queen required workers to clock out and *then* wait for our bag checks. We regularly waited several minutes. This form of theft isn't unique to fast fashion. Over the past few years, class-action lawsuits against several major retailers—Ralph Lauren, Gap, Banana Republic, Nike, Big Lots, Ulta, Amazon, and Starbucks—have sought wages lost while waiting for loss prevention inspections.[15] The California Supreme

Court decided in favor of Apple workers in 2020, after "Apple argued that the searches, while mandatory, were not required if employees simply did not bring bags to work."[16]

Class-action lawsuits against hotel and grocery chains in Illinois—one of the few states with regulation on biometric data collection—question the legality of fingerprint scanners too. The suit claims the employers failed to acquire written consent for the collection of biometric data and did not disclose how long such data would be stored nor how it would be destroyed. "Unlike, say, a stolen company ID, which can be replaced, individuals can't order up a new body part, raising concerns about what could happen if scans of their fingertips' arches, loops, and whorls fell into the wrong hands."[17] Despite the growing ubiquity of fingerprint scanning in everyday life—fingerprints commonly unlock personal cell phones, for example—among retail workers, biometric fingerprint scanners reinforced the idea that workers were always already potential criminals. Engaging with biometric systems cues bodily reactions (hearts racing, palms sweating), while their failure exacerbates anxieties of an already hectic environment. These battles over time theft, wage theft, and biometric data raise the question: *Who is really stealing from whom?*

Like many other worker-monitoring technologies, fingerprint scanning has long-standing connections to military and policing. As feminist surveillance studies scholar Shoshana Magnet explains, rudimentary fingerprint scanning technology first appeared in Wall Street investment firms as a time-clock mechanism.[18] These scanners were put on the market by the company Identimation, which was acquired in the 1990s by Wackenhut, now known as G4S, one of the world's largest private security companies. G4S has been criticized for its involvement in torturing Palestinian prisoners in Israel, operating private prisons in the United States, and working with Dakota Access against protestors in Standing Rock, North Dakota.[19] The acquisition of Identimation by Wackenhut/G4S should come as no surprise, as police and prisons have advanced biometric fingerprinting technology perhaps more than any other industry. Magnet writes that "prisoners themselves represented 'acres of skin' to a biometric industry in its infancy, and one requiring a broad population upon which to test its products."[20] By finding new uses in retail, fingerprint scanning returns to its workplace origins.

Point-of-Sale Surveillance: "You Know We Track That, Right?"

Even after clocking in, employees continue to be monitored as they move throughout the store. In my fieldwork, this happened most extensively at the point of sale.

As I described in the previous chapter, working at the cash register is one of the most exasperating duties for an entry-level fast-fashion retail employee. Lines grow long, sensors beep at multiple registers simultaneously, and music blares, making it difficult to think straight, let alone check out customers quickly, efficiently, and with a pleasant demeanor. As Zarina shared in the previous chapter, "[the cash register] was a little more stressful because the lineups would be constant. . . . Deal with one customer, they make a $300 purchase, then deal with another customer."

At the beginning of each shift, workers logged into the register's computer system, and with this information, computer programs could then generate performance reports based on aggregate-level data, while also identifying individual transactions. The retail industry has dubbed this approach "exception-based reporting." The software flags workers who, for instance, might be taking too long to complete transactions or have logged a suspiciously high number of customer returns.

According to the company RetailNext, which produces the software illustrated in figure 4.2, "high risk" transactions are marked with a dot. Each transaction is matched with corresponding surveillance video and receipts. Some versions of the dashboard summarize information at the company and store level, pinpointing "highest risk stores" and "highest risk cashiers."

This platform is sold to retailers on not only its accuracy but its efficiency. According to its website, "Just like that—what used to take all morning now takes a couple of clicks. . . . It's not only easier for the LP [loss

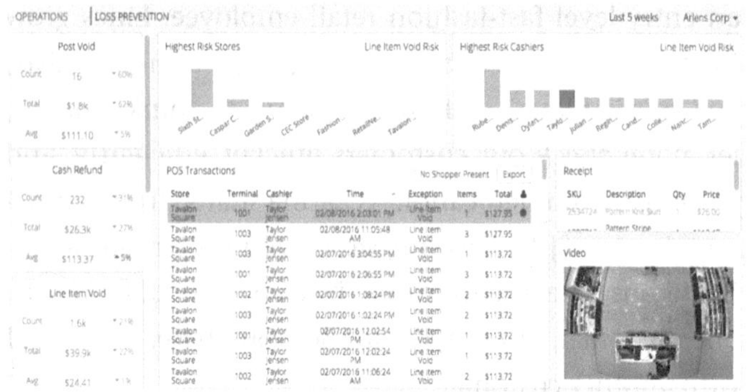

Figure 4.2
Exception-based reporting dashboard. *Source:* RetailNext.net.

prevention] professional, but it allows increasingly tight personnel resources and budgets to be allocated more efficiently, more effectively."[21] Such software automates retail management, combining new and previously distinct sets of information to identify company-level trends as well as mark individual employees as suspicious. Since managers or loss prevention personnel cannot track every single employee, now exception-based reporting does the heavy lifting.

Retail industry statistics claim that "internal theft" by employees accounts for around 30 percent of total loss.[22] Richard Hollinger, a criminologist who studies "employee dishonesty" and helps administer the National Retail Security Survey, told *Loss Prevention Magazine* that employers might reduce internal theft by providing workers with "increased hours and increased wages . . . They want jobs that pay well. And that's still a problem with retail, where many retail employees are still paid minimum wage."[23]

Hollinger's insights are not widely shared, though: a flyer I picked up at the NRF Protect conference for Gunnebo Cash Management Solutions, an automated money counting system, warns: "Shrinkage is not just a problem for your rivals. Globally for example, recent surveys show that retailers lose $128.5 billion in cash a year, with almost one-third due to internal theft and an additional 20% due to error. *When you are hiring students or other temporary and inexperienced workers, shrinkage can become a headache*" (emphasis mine). For companies like Gunnebo, the solution is to provide not more stable jobs or better wages, but increased automation and surveillance.

Often, when I would ask my interviewees about how their cashier performance was tracked, they immediately noted the presence of security cameras. Only upon further pressing did they reflect on the role of automated surveillance. I commonly had exchanges like the following one with Elijah.

M: Would you log into the register with your employee card or something?

Elijah: No, you have a PIN and your employee number so a six- or seven-digit code, it might be up to seven now. Seven-digit code, type in a PIN that you set.

M: And why did you do that? Do you know?

Elijah: Why did we do that versus [what]? That's just what the system was.

M: Do you know why they had people log in?

Elijah: I guess so they can say, if you make a mistake, it's on you. Or if a customer got double charged, it's on *you*.

Elijah's comment of "that's just what the system was" reveals the extent to which various forms of surveillance have become a normalized aspect of work and life in the twenty-first century, especially in cities like New York.[24] While Elijah understands this monitoring as an everyday part of the job, he simultaneously concludes that its ultimate objective is to place additional burden on employees; as he emphasized, "It's on *you*."

Though often invisible, digital point-of-sale monitoring can have detrimental impacts on low-wage workers. During my cash register training at McFashion, a current employee told me and my fellow trainees about a button to correct transactions, which she said we could use as often as necessary. When she said this, our floor manager spun to her, blurting, "You know we track that, right?" The employee's eyes grew wide in distress. In another case, one of my interviewees, Jesse, had worked at McFashion in Los Angeles. He told me that he once put five dollars—half an hour's wages—from his own pocket into the register when his drawer came up short; being reprimanded for previous mistakes, he said, had been "terrifying." Similarly, Elijah told me: "The rule with them is, if you're under anything more than $75, it's automatic termination. If you have someone under $40 it might not be their fault. It's an honest, slight mistake. But they'd still fire them because they'd see it as they'd have the potential to do it again."

These examples from Jesse and Elijah illustrate how worker monitoring can increase workers' sense of insecurity in a context of big data surveillance: while they might not be aware of exactly how they are being monitored, they know being even a few dollars off is a risk they can't afford to take, especially when they are both trying to pay their way through school and their labor power is easily replaceable.

While surveillance proliferates at the point of sale, employees find ways to adapt. Jesse shares, "Learning all the codes [for clothes] was very important. You know I was really fast at getting customers in and out, in and out. And if I made a small mistake I would just, like, not do anything about it, and just get it done. That was really important in the holiday season to keep our lines down." Maintaining the flow of customers was essential in this setting, since long lines tend to stoke customer dissatisfaction, which frontline workers must bear the brunt of. When I asked Jesse to provide a specific example of tricks he used to help keep the lines flowing, he said he would enter technically valid, but inaccurate, information at the cash register: "A lot of times the clothes wouldn't scan in, so you'd have to type in the code. I'd type in the code and, you know, it would not really give me anything, or I'll search and I'll pick and choose. Like, oh I'll just pick this shirt 'cause it has the same design on it, you know?"

Surveillance scholar Gary Marx calls behavior like Jesse's a "distorting move."[25] Put another way, the code Jesse punched to ring up a particular garment was incorrect, but it was close enough to allow him to keep lines moving. It was a small workaround to game the system. Jesse was additionally required to solicit customers' personal email addresses, which he sometimes avoided by entering his own instead: "The funny thing is I've put in my email a thousand times." While I laughed along, this anecdote highlights an important dynamic. Distorting moves here operated less as a conscious form of resistance than as a survival mechanism in this sped-up, hyper-surveilled, and undercompensated line of work.

At the cash register, fast-paced work is monitored intermittently by managers who count the drawers, as well as continuously and visibly by video cameras, and continuously but invisibly by digital point-of-sale monitoring. Most employees had spent little time reflecting on this digital surveillance, but when they did, they appeared startled or were resigned to the reality that it made their work more stressful and more unstable.

Analog Threads

My own work experiences and observations at the NRF Protect conference made it seem like digital tools reigned supreme. However, my interview with Ryan reminded me of an important point.

M: Can you tell me, when you come to work, how do you clock in and track your time and stuff like that?

Ryan: First of all, when you come in, you get a separate door. It's the side door. We leave and we get checked out from that door. It's efficient because it's away from customers and not distracting them or making noise. Psychological noise and stuff like that.

M: What do you mean?

Ryan: I guess, like, if you see people being pat down, customers are gonna be like, what's going on here? And that might, like, mess up their shopping. So that's what I mean, just like noise and stuff like that, anything that could distract the customer. So, you come in, you leave by that door and you get pat down.

M: They pat down your body?

Ryan: They just check your bag and stuff like that. They don't pat you down or anything. Let's see, so you go upstairs and there's this back door. The back door goes to an office, the break room, and the lockers room. So, you go back there, and there's two computers, so you clock in with those. We have this thing called Kronos. We clock in from there.

My initial question about how Ryan clocks in was intended to focus on digital surveillance. But before we even got to that point, Ryan described analog forms of tracking and control. At his store, workers entered a side door where they clocked in and out and had their belongings searched. The fact that Ryan chose the phrase *pat down* indicates the sense of being treated as a potential criminal. The employees, if not the customers, endured this criminalization, which creates, in his words, *psychological noise*.

Only after these analog examples does Ryan move on to Kronos' digital timekeeping. Ryan's comments highlight how new technologies don't necessarily wipe out older practices. Retailers rely on both digital and analog tools and techniques, treating workers as suspicious, traceable, and replaceable.

How Data Fashions Precarity

Surveillance and retail work have long gone hand in hand. Putting my findings against the backdrop of historical research and more recent sociological studies of retail labor reveals how methods of surveillance tend to shift alongside the retail labor process. I've illustrated these general trends in table 4.1.

In early twentieth-century department store contexts, workers were trained to engage in skilled selling, and managers expected deep engagement with customers. Historian Susan Porter Benson describes department store sales-floor discipline as too often "all stick and no carrot."[26] Her book *Counter Cultures: Saleswomen, Managers, and Customers in American Department*

Table 4.1
Retail labor processes and surveillance

Store model	Labor process	Surveillance method
Department store	Skilled selling	Managerial oversight
Branded apparel	Deskilled emotional labor	Secret shoppers
Fast fashion	Just-in-time retail	Digital surveillance

Stores, 1890–1940 includes archival photos from women's magazines depicting salesgirls congregating in small groups, sharing gossip or grievances while a male figure—presumably either "store detective, spying floor manager, [or] undercover agent"[27]—lingers ominously in the background. Physical presence implied visual oversight and direct discipline.

The shift from department store to the proliferation of branded apparel retail chains (such as the Gap, Abercrombie & Fitch, and The Limited) led to deskilled affective labor. More important than knowing the product was providing a positive and formulaic interaction to customers.[28] As I discussed in the previous chapter, sociologist Arlie Hochschild coined the term "emotional labor" in this era to capture how corporations make money from the management of human feeling. Workers sold not just a product, but a service and an experience. Later, sociologist Ashley Mears applied the term "aesthetic labor" to how workers cultivate a specific look and way of being; they indeed embody the brand.[29] Abercrombie & Fitch customers, for instance, may have easily identified the workers: not only are they greeted with standard phrases, but the workers also have a certain *Abercrombie & Fitch–ness* about them. Workers looked, sounded, and acted as if they belonged.

In those contexts, shopkeepers no longer visually tracked every worker, and interventions such as secret shoppers helped keep modern retail employees in line. These undercover customers could appear unannounced at any moment and were usually hired through a third party. After each shopping trip, secret shoppers produced quantitative evaluations based on the service they received, thus creating a threat of surveillance without constant supervision. Vicky Osterweil writes, "Mystery shoppers are miniature thought police, affective pinkertons, mercenary management to whom real management outsources the legwork of everyday psychic control."[30] Mystery shoppers ensured standardization of service, affect, and appearance of branded retail workers.

In recent years, however, big data, digital surveillance, and fast fashion have altered the terms of retail labor. Following my argument in the previous chapter, the primary tasks of fast-fashion retail work require more "material" than immaterial labor—with carrying, folding, and sorting a constantly changing stream of stuff being of the utmost import. One former employee I talked to said, "I've shopped here for years. I have never really felt like I've ever once been, like, serviced here, to be really honest with you. Mystery shoppers would probably benefit their business, but at the same time I almost feel like this store is such a vehicle for money they almost just don't care." As customer service takes a back seat to the work of maintaining a nonstop flow of goods, the need for "affective pinkertons" in the form of mystery shoppers wanes. Worker behavior, like everything else in the store, becomes more easily tracked by technology. If mystery shoppers were the *affective pinkertons* of yesteryear, new technologies make up today's *digital pinkertons.*

Surveillance scholar Mark Andrejevic discusses how these trends in surveillance automation exist within a broader social shift from discipline to preemption.[31] He writes, "If subjects cannot be relied on to discipline themselves, then surveillance must become as comprehensive as possible. However, this level of monitoring requires automation of both data collection and data processing (and, eventually, of response)."[32] Popularized in the blockbuster science-fiction crime film *Minority Report,* the idea of stopping criminals before they act is now commonplace. Law enforcement, for example, regularly relies on digital technologies to *predict* which geographic areas and populations are most "at risk" of committing a crime. These practices have been subject to much critique, including for how they deepen surveillance and criminalization of already heavily policed places and people.[33] Similarly, Virginia Eubanks's book *Automating Inequality* illustrates how automated data collection punishes poor people in everyday life, at child welfare agencies, housing organizations, and other social services that should ostensibly help, not hurt, the poor.[34] Retail companies have jumped on this bandwagon, with significant consequences for their low-wage workers.

The National Retail Federation's 2020 National Retail Security Survey, which collected information from sixty-nine retailers, reflects these shifts. "Respondents say their organizations are devoting more resources to fight shrink in the coming year, with a majority of those enhancements coming in technology investments."[35] One chart tracks "biggest year-over-year movement" in retail security. Mystery shoppers, secured display fixtures, and static observation booths or mirrors are waning. Tactics on the upswing include live customer-visible CCTV, point-of-sale exception-based interfaces (such as the cashier tracking I described earlier in this chapter), and internet protocol analytics. In other words, analog surveillance is out. Digital is in.

In the new world of retail, technoscience helps normalize surveillance and exacerbate inequality. The growth of software used to automate employee schedules not only creates new norms of short shifts and fluctuating employee calendars, but also encourages employers to engage in additional forms of automated control. In settings where the employees turn over as quickly as the store inventory, the propensity to treat workers like potential criminals becomes amplified.

Applicants might be screened out by databases before they are even interviewed. If hired, their managers might follow them on social media, further extending the reach of surveillance beyond the workplace. Biometric fingerprinting purports to provide objective time keeping for today's "modern" (i.e., flexible) workforce by preventing time theft and buddy punching, while software that tracks and aggregates cash register transactions encourages employers to quickly pinpoint "exceptions" within a large pool of cashiers, exerting more pressure on an already stressful task. Meanwhile, loss prevention staff are encouraged to take their local police chiefs out to lunch.

The preceding few chapters document the nature of just-in-time retail labor, as well as how these spaces have become sites of everyday resistance. In the next chapter, we'll zoom out, looking at how social movements have engaged retail as a site for collective organizing.

5
Retail Disruptions: Confronting Digital Surveillance

I was heading into Manhattan for the action commemorating the one-year anniversary of the killing of Eric Garner, so I figured I should stop by McFashion, where I was working at the time.[1] Even though computer software used sophisticated algorithms to fine-tune our weekly schedules to mirror shopper demand, somehow no formal platform existed for workers to check their hours online. Once inside the store, I darted through packs of roving customers, past cramped clothing racks, and down two flights of a congested escalator to reach the break room. About fifteen of my coworkers slumped on metal folding chairs, taking a brief respite from the hours of standing, sorting clothes, and appeasing entitled tourists. I found my name among the hundreds listed on the bulletin board; the automated scheduler had assigned me eighteen hours for the following week, broken into four shifts. Like nearly all my coworkers, I was encouraged to provide open schedule availability even though the job was part-time. I typed my hours into my iPhone, weaseled my way out of the store, and walked north from Times Square to meet the other demonstrators at Columbus Circle.

After the requisite speeches, the crowd took the streets, with hundreds of us marching through Central Park and making our way down Sixth Avenue. Together, we repeatedly shouted, "I can't breathe": the infamous phrase Garner yelled eleven times at the Staten Island police who attacked and killed him for selling loose cigarettes. The demonstration culminated in a die-in in the middle of Herald Square, under the glowing lights of the recently opened, world's largest H&M. Police stood at the ready, batons in hand, while shoppers weaved through the unusually dense crowd.

While I had participated in other protests that went through major shopping centers, something about this one felt especially significant. Maybe it's because this was the first time I related to an area simultaneously as protester, consumer, and worker. Garner died in part because he labored in the informal economy in a working-class Staten Island neighborhood—a prime target in an era of predictive policing. He was punished for being structurally surplus to capital and "daring to survive."[2] In other words, as much Black studies scholarship makes clear, the U.S. prison system is closely intertwined with a racial political economy; poor people and people of color who attempt to make a life for themselves outside the formal economy are deemed a threat to the social order.[3] Ramsey Orta had wielded his own phone as a powerful weapon, documenting

Garner's death for all to see; despite the footage, Garner's killer, Officer Daniel Pantaleo, would still roam free. The protest at Herald Square also took place at a nexus of capitalism, surveillance, and precarious labor.

I wondered, How does the world of fast fashion relate to broader interconnected but distinct struggles for racial, gender, and economic justice?

Fast-fashion retail labor and state-sanctioned police violence seem at first glance fundamentally distinct from one another, informed by different logics and requiring unique responses. Yet, in participating in Black Lives Matter protests in and around retail spaces, hearing how other people related to the Movement for Black Lives, and volunteering at a retail workers' center, I noted how often these struggles converged. First, they overlapped spatially and temporally, with Black Lives Matter protests regularly targeting retail spaces across the United States during the time of my fieldwork. They additionally overlapped demographically, with many of my coworkers comprising the same populations targeted by police violence, and many of my comrades organizing against both unjust working conditions and unjust policing.

The digital connections between retail labor and anti-police organizing stem from their entanglement with what a group of scholars at the Precarity Lab at the University of Michigan call *technoprecarity*, which points to "how digital technologies amplify conditions of exploitation." Their analysis encourages scholars to think about how surveillance impacts *which people* and with *what consequences*.

Take the case of policing. The insatiable hunger for data has direct implications for who gets caught up in the criminal legal system. Sarah Brayne's research with the Los Angeles police department shows how data moves across institutional contexts for purposes of profit and control. With big data policing, people who already exist within heavily surveilled populations are now even more likely to be tracked by law enforcement systems even if they have not committed any crimes. In one of several examples, Brayne describes efforts to compile information across law enforcement, social services, health services, mental health services, and child and family services into one master database.[4] Just by utilizing social services, people are now likely to be in law enforcement databases as well, even if they haven't committed any crime. Meanwhile, the tech companies that power these big data solutions stand to profit enormously. This is just one way that our current data-driven economy disproportionately impacts the poor and working classes.

As I learned at the NRF Protect conference described in the previous chapter, a huge and growing variety of surveillance technologies that already have their hold in law enforcement are now being marketed to retailers. In this chapter, I explore how just-in-time retail labor connects to broader movements for racial, gender, and economic justice. I draw on my participation in and interviews with key activists in two social movements that created a political presence in and around just-in-time retail spaces between 2014 and 2017: the Black Lives Matter (BLM) movement and a workers' center called the Retail Action Project (RAP). These two movements, while employing at times vastly different tactics and demands, help advance a *critical data praxis* by organizing around the role of technology in perpetuating inequalities.

For both RAP and BLM, I provide an overview of the organization/movement and describe two illustrative snapshots. For RAP, I examine a direct action at the National Retail Federation's annual conference and exhibition hall where vendors peddled their latest retail technologies. For BLM, I focus on the 2014 and 2015 protests at the Mall of America in Minneapolis, Minnesota, which presented some of the most dramatic attacks against the nexus of consumer capitalism, digital surveillance, and policing.

The work of both the Retail Action Project and Black Lives Matter is informed by long legacies of struggle—including but not limited to labor organizing among marginalized workers as well as battles for Black power and against white supremacy.[5] While those histories inform this chapter, I would be remiss to claim that I adequately engage those rich legacies here; such an attempt would require another book project entirely. Nevertheless, I contend that the following comparison illustrates how, just as technologies of worker exploitation and surveillance have transformed in the digital age, so too have movements for collective liberation.

The Retail Action Project

In the mid-twentieth-century era of department stores and the rise of mass consumption, several factors conspired against the unionization of retail workers, including high employee turnover, staunchly anti-union retail managers, and paternalistic union organizers. Given these circumstances, historian Susan Porter Benson writes, "it is remarkable not how little but how often saleswomen tried to organize."[6] Several of the aforementioned conditions, especially worker turnover, continue to hinder unionization today. Between 1983 and 2013, retail worker unionization shrank from 11 percent to a mere 4.6 percent. The rate of union density in the apparel industry is lower than almost all other retail sectors, at a mere 0.7 percent (department stores boast 2.4 percent, while grocery stores are among the most highly organized at over 15 percent).[7]

The Retail Action Project (RAP), according to its website, "is a member-based organization with the mission of building worker power, elevating industry standards, and promoting family-sustaining jobs. We achieve this through engaging in collective action, highlighting worker voices, growing workers' professional capacity, and nurturing member leadership." RAP is a part of a coalition of workers' centers, which are growing increasingly common in New York City and across the United States.[8]

Labor unions and workers' centers have historically shared a somewhat antagonistic relationship. Part of a long trajectory of nonunion worker organizing, workers' centers attempt to provide services and act as a hub for community organizing for flexible and often largely immigrant workforces in an era of austerity and low union membership. The first workers' centers emerged in the 1970s in New York, North Carolina, South Carolina, Texas, and California among Black, Latinx, and Asian immigrant workers, with numbers growing in succeeding waves in response to new immigrant workforces. As of 2007, there were at least 160 workers' centers across the United States. According to critics, workers centers' campaigns against wage theft may prevent more "offensive" organizing, while reliance on foundation funding rather than union dues hinders long-term institutionalization. In addition, some argue that workers' centers' practice of community building and small, workplace-based campaigns contrasts with union's attempts at "large-scale industry-based" campaigns.[9]

On top of that, although women of color are now more likely to be union members than any other demographic group,[10] fast-fashion retail organizing is enmeshed in long tensions over race, gender, and sexuality in the labor movement. Throughout U.S. civil rights struggles—including the March on Washington, the Memphis sanitation workers' strike, and the Poor People's Campaign—many mainstream labor organizations remained absent if not adversarial.[11] Revolutionary union movements of the 1970s saw mainstream unions like the United Auto Workers "as equally oppressive" in furthering managerial interests, work speedups, and racial hierarchies.[12] Similar difficulties mark the trajectory of LGBTQ union movement.[13]

RAP's worker center is commended for organizing "queer class and race" issues.[14] One of RAP's key features was its Member Organizing Training program, which provides a small stipend and political education for interested retail workers. Ben, a RAP organizer and former member organizer in training, said, "The program consisted of me thinking more about my community, who I am as a person, the nation, capitalism, white supremacy, all of the things." Rachel, who was RAP's executive director, told me a commitment to understanding these connections underpins the organization as a whole:

> Workers are part of an ecosystem and as workers it's important to have a very well-rounded understanding of all the different factors at play, versus when we talk about just "our jobs." Race and gender, you know, everything that we do is political from the second we wake up to the second we close our eyes. It's been fascinating to have members come in the door and be like, "Yeah, you know, I don't do politics." And to be able to say, "Yeah, you know you do it every day. Every single day. In fact, your very existence is deeply political." Our work has to be grounded in that idea.

Rachel explained that, in this way, a RAP member's work doesn't stop even when they've won their workplace organizing campaign. There are always more opportunities to fight for justice.

The Retail Action Project differs from other worker centers in that it was created out of the Retail, Wholesale and Department Store Union. RWDSU was founded in the late 1930s in New York City but generally stagnated following "anti-Communist tension after the passage of the Taft-Hartley Act."[15] RAP emerged in 2005 through a partnership between the RWDSU and a tenants' rights organization called the Good Old Lower East Side.[16] RAP organized small, independent retailers in Manhattan's SoHo shopping district, targeting a store called Yellow Rat Bastard for wage violations. It launched similar campaigns at Shoemania, Scoop NYC, and Mystique Boutique. RAP attempts to exert force on the retail industry by providing service training to help workers forge a sense of occupational identity, holding hiring events to "control labor supply"[17] and allocating benefits based on organizational membership rather than location or focusing on a specific work site.

When large retailers and fast-fashion chains began to proliferate throughout the city, RAP's organizing strategy shifted. Robyn, who had been an organizer with RAP for a year and a half when I interviewed her, said, "RAP has definitely changed in a sense, but so has the retail industry. . . . I think RAP had a hold of the retail industry when it was smaller in the city. Of course,

SoHo was huge, and like Fifth Avenue, maybe Herald Square a little bit, but [the industry] wasn't this much. So [RAP] had it on lock. But now the industry is so insidious and prominent, bringing in so much money." That insidiousness is what we've seen throughout this book: stores across the city with unreliable employee schedules that are determined by algorithms, intensified daily workloads, and widespread worker monitoring and surveillance.

These shifting labor conditions make organizing exceedingly difficult. Emma, a former RAP organizer, told me, "I organized retail workers for three and a half years and honestly turnover was the hardest thing I faced while organizing retail workers in general. Because I would meet awesome people that had so much potential, but they just couldn't take it anymore." With the rise of fast fashion, high turnover was coupled with a large employee base. Emma explained: "You also need more organizers if you have over a hundred employees you're trying to organize. Versus when you have forty you may just need two organizers." Emma learned this lesson the hard way. When RAP launched a campaign against Zara in 2015, four organizers covered seven different locations across the city. "We got burnt the fuck out." These conditions took their toll on Emma and other RAP organizers, demanding as much flexibility and overwork from them as from frontline retail employees.

As I have elucidated throughout the previous chapters, digital technology and just-in-time production processes facilitated these changes in the labor force. RAP would attempt to confront some of these issues head-on at the annual meeting of the National Retail Federation.

Snapshot: RAP at NRF's Big Show

Ben, dressed in all black, pulled the dark ski mask over his face. "Man, I didn't sign up for this!" he shouted. About twenty of us had just left the RAP office near Penn Station, walking down the blustery Manhattan streets that frigid January morning. Ben's ski mask served less to protect his anonymity than to shield him from the sub-freezing temperatures. It was Martin Luther King Day, and political rallies were planned across the city; the holiday carried extra weight that year following the ongoing wave of Black Lives Matter protests throughout New York City and across the country. But before any of us headed to those events, we had another task before us.

"Where exactly are we going again?" I asked one of the labor organizers shuffling next to me. "It's the biggest meeting of all the retailers, where they talk about all the latest technology and stuff." That was putting it lightly. We were headed to a meeting of the National Retail Federation (NRF), the world's largest retail trade association known for generating industry projections (many journalistic investigations of the retail industry cite numbers generated by NRF, for example) and lobbying in favor of corporate interests. NRF holds conferences throughout the year, and in the previous chapter I describe my trip to its "loss prevention" conference, NRF Protect. But the federation's most well-known and widely attended event is the Big Show, held each January. In 2016, the Big Show hosted 35,000 attendees and nearly 600 exhibitors at the sprawling Jacob Javits Center on Manhattan's West Side.

We finally made it to 11th Avenue, where we met up with those who had taxied over with their picket signs and banners. "We need to spread out!" someone yelled. I asked one of the organizers what the plan was once inside. She said a few people were going to do a banner drop (which usually entails unveiling a banner in a highly visible location) and a mic check (in which one person will yell a statement or chant, and the group will repeat it in unison, thereby creating a "human microphone"), and the other volunteers and I were there to support the mic check and do chants.

I followed the crowd inside the glass complex, and most of the group scampered off. I introduced myself to two young women, RAP volunteers like myself, who stood close to each other in awe. "This is so weird," one said, stuffing her hands in her oversized puffer jacket. Huge corporate banners hung all around the periphery, emblazoned with logos of giants like American Express, IBM, and Starbucks or business-ese slogans such as, "Be More Productive with Every Step." Meanwhile, white-collar professionals zipped about, presumably networking as they rushed from corporate exhibits to breakout conference sessions. We followed others in our group up the escalator, where we noticed more of "our people" already staked out, dressed in business casual, and blending into the buzzing cafeteria overlooking the main floor. An organizer discretely distributed fake lanyards. "They're blank, so just hide them under your jackets." Robyn told me, "I was here for Comic Con last year, and this is way more intense. I guess the only difference is that people aren't in costume." I responded, "Oh, they're in costume, just a different kind." Robyn turned to me with a grin, "Right, a different kind of costume."

Then we heard it. "Mic check! Mic check!"

"Here we go!" someone shouted. I tossed my banana peel in the garbage, wove my way through suited men, and tried to get close enough to the protestors to hear the chants. Although the plan was to spread out more to make the chants echo, our voices were dampened by the center's sprawling size, so we instead stayed close together. Two organizers, proudly donning bright red Retail Action Project bandanas around their faces, dropped a banner reading "Retail Workers Need $15/HR & Full Time" over the edge of the balcony.

Together we chanted, "Nine an hour, it's time to fight the power!" and "Unite! To fight! This minimum wage is not all right!"

I looked around me, nervous about what I might observe. There were a lot of people filming, including RAP participants and conference attendees alike, and I was happy that people seemed to be paying attention. Within a few short minutes, security approached and told us to leave. We quickly cooperated, picking up the banner and making our way down the escalator. We continued to chant as we slowly marched out. Outside, we joined a few others in the group, who held large cutout letters spelling "WE HAVE A DREAM."

Critical Data Praxis in the Labor Movement

That day at the Javits Center, I made small talk with some of the union organizers about the rise of automated scheduling, the makers of which were surely present at the NRF conference. I rarely noticed discussions of data-driven labor management in conversations between organizers and members or frontline employees, perhaps because the technology remained largely invisible to frontline workers. Yet, clearly, technology played a key component in the climate in which RAP engaged.

At first, I got the impression that RAP was simplifying the terrain. But in volunteering with the Retail Action Project for over a year, I came to learn that what the organization wanted of the industry was much more complex than that. Organizers and activists did not simply desire full-time, stable schedules. Rather, in this age of technoprecarity, they fought for technology deployed in the interests of workers, not corporations. I spoke with Rachel, RAP's director at that time, about these issues. She said:

> When you hear the flowery talk about [automated schedulers like] Kronos and how this is a win-win for the employer and the employee, you would imagine that it—almost you know—creates this image of managers and all of their employees sitting down at the close of the week to figure out what the next two weeks look like, and inputting availability into this software and popping out this incredible schedule. The truth is, that's not how it works at all. The software is used to track peak sales and then provide the scheduling manager with a base or minimal number of staff needed to cover how many people might come into the store. There's no conversation with employees.

Acknowledging that technology is never neutral, but rather an instrument of power, Rachel also praised New York City's 2017 ban—which RAP and RWDSU lobbied heavily in favor of—of on-call scheduling as a method of combating this "temporal inequality"[18] and shifting the scales in favor of workers' interests.

Clearly, contemporary retail labor organizing needs to take seriously how technology exacerbates exploitation, as RAP does. In the years since I conducted this research, RWDSU has been active in organizing Whole Foods and Amazon workers, where technology is an even more overt threat to worker health and well-being.[19]

As I described in the previous chapter, many of the same technologies involved in digitally managing and monitoring workers, and several of which were on display at the NRF Big Show and NRF Protect, are found or were pioneered in policing and military contexts. It might not come as a surprise, then, that during my fieldwork, RAP was not the only group targeting the retail industry as a site of political struggle.

Disrupting Business as Usual: Black Lives Matter in Retail Space

The Movement for Black Lives stemmed from a long lineage of struggles against the carceral and police state, especially after the murder of Trayvon Martin by vigilante George Zimmerman in 2012, and erupted into a nationwide movement following the killing of Michael Brown by police officer Darren Wilson in 2014 in Ferguson, Missouri. The Black Lives Matter hashtag originated from queer Black activist Alicia Garza, along with Patrisse Cullors and Opal [Ayọ] Tometi.[20] In this chapter, when I talk about Black Lives Matter, I'm talking about not only the hashtag or the foundation, but the broader movement, including an array of organizations and actors who regularly block freeways, occupy police stations, and disrupt everyday life, calling for everything from police reform and punishment of police misconduct to police and prison abolition. In many ways, the movement represents the twenty-first-century iteration of a decades-long battle between politicians, nonprofit organizations, celebrities, professional organizers, academics, and activists.[21]

At first, it seemed like Black Lives Matter's focus on shopping centers was simply a matter of timing. Since Darren Wilson's non-indictment in 2014 closely preceded the holiday season, it made sense that protesters would disrupt the Macy's Thanksgiving Day Parade,[22] hold nationwide protests on Black Friday,[23] and conduct die-ins at retail giants H&M and Forever 21.[24] Over the course of 2015, though, retail spaces continued to be a key protest target, including Black Friday actions in Chicago, New York City, Los Angeles, Portland, and Seattle, as well as a national call to boycott Black Friday altogether. The *Chicago Tribune* reports that protests cost stores 25–50 percent of Black Friday sales.[25] In Maryland, Mondawmin Mall served as ground zero for the 2015 Baltimore riots, when police shut down the local bus system and stoked the anger of Black youth who gathered at the space following the funeral of Freddie Gray, who died in police custody.[26] In an interview with *PBS NewsHour*, historian N. D. B. Connolly commented:

> This mall is where the riots began [on April 27]. It's the Mondawmin Mall, here in Northwest Baltimore. It's just across from Frederick Douglass High School, and it actually sits in the middle of three big narratives about the city's history. One is the most recent riot. The second is the story of prices and the everyday life of living in Baltimore and what this mall represents for everyday people trying to shop here. And the third is that this mall actually began as one of the city's first shopping malls that used to primarily serve white customers. And it suffered white flight and had to

> basically repurpose itself to deal with a black clientele. And so, the history of segregation, the history of price gouging, and the more recent history of the riot are all built here, around the Mondawmin Mall.[27]

Connolly's interview points to the social and political history of retail.

Indeed, as historian Traci Parker demonstrates in her book *Department Stores and the Black Freedom Movement*, retail was central to the twentieth-century civil rights movement, creating a nexus of struggle around labor and consumption. Depression-era "Don't Buy Where You Can't Work" campaigns—which responded to widespread layoffs of African Americans following the stock market crash—set the groundwork for department store movements of the 1930s and 1940s. Many campaigns in this movement promoted fair hiring practices and pushed against discrimination and segregation of consumers. During this era, multiple riots—including those in Detroit and Harlem in 1943—saw looting of white-owned or openly discriminatory businesses. Parker argues that the metamorphosis of retail from high-end department stores to mega shopping malls and super-centers was not based on economics alone. The move from public downtown shopping districts to privately owned suburban spaces attempted to squash retail's political potential.[28]

That transformation was, according to urban theorist Mike Davis, "an especially disturbing guide to the emerging liaisons between urban architecture and the police state."[29] At the neighborhood level, malls, department stores, and shopping areas are key nodes of capitalist restructuring, regularly justifying sweeping gentrification.[30] Keeping these areas safe and clean for consumers—meaning free of those deemed dangerous or surplus—often relies on quality-of-life policing, which leads to increased incarceration, police violence, and death.[31] Each day I exited the subway to work in Manhattan, I encountered NYPD vans, cruisers, and mobile surveillance towers, highlighting so clearly the non-spectacular, mundane ways in which twenty-first century policing and consumer capitalism go hand in hand.

Stores also overtly profile shoppers, utilizing the police's stop-and-frisk tactic to protect these sanctified sites of consumption. In 2015, Zara faced ridicule when a survey by the Center for Popular Democracy revealed they used the term "special order" to verbally mark suspicious customers; 46 percent of workers surveyed claimed that "Black customers were called special orders 'always' or 'often.'"[32] One of my interviewees agreed: "I'm sure you're aware but loss prevention was a lot of times a pretty racialized thing. Keep your eyes on the Black girl dressed a certain way. Or Black girls period." As I discussed in the last chapter, workers themselves are regularly criminalized, subjected to bag checks, and tracked through biometric monitoring and big data surveillance.

Digital policing and surveillance have not replaced human control, but evolve alongside it.[33] Other scholars note that digital surveillance is itself a form of profiling, by sorting human bodies into discrete categories.[34] We should not be surprised by these connections, given that algorithms contain the biases of humans who create them.[35] These combinations of crudeness and sophistication, of analog and digital methods of capture and collective refusal, can be seen in actions against the BLM movement. Arguably, one of the most dramatic politicizations of retail occurred at the Mall of America.

#BlackChristmas: BLM at MOA

The Mall of America was erected in 1992 in Bloomington, Minnesota, just outside Minneapolis, and while it is no longer the largest mall in the United States—Philadelphia's King of Prussia Mall now claims that title at 2.9 million square feet—it remains significant for several reasons. In the words of Jonathan Sterne, "The Mall's utter extremity on one hand and everydayness on the other offer a unique perspective on a place where consumerism is conflated with nationalism."[36] These days, the megamall represents both an apex of leisure consumption and a quickly dying breed, as malls across the country continue to fail amid the rise of online retailing.[37] But with the Mall of America's unique success, it has transformed alongside the rest of the retail industry. Forever 21 grew to a staggering 80,000 square feet when it took over the former space of Bloomingdale's in 2012, and a two-story Zara opened in 2016 to wide acclaim.

The megamall is additionally notable for its security apparatus. According to a profile in *Foreign Policy*, "unlike many other retail establishments, which hire inexperienced rent-a-cops to enforce security, the Mall of America has its own antiterrorism task force."[38] In a 2008 testimony given at the U.S. House of Representatives' Committee on Homeland Security's hearing, "The Challenge of Protecting Mass Gatherings in a Post-9/11 World," Douglas Reynolds, director of security for the Mall, said that "because of the sheer number of visitors to the Mall of America and our status as a symbol of consumerism and capitalism, security remains a top priority for us." The Mall's role as a symbol of both national pride and conspicuous consumption justifies excessive surveillance.

One of the Mall's most well-known programs, Risk Assessment and Mitigation (RAM), relies on an Israeli technique called "behavior profiling," which purportedly locates and intervenes in suspicious behavior; RAM leaders are trained directly in Israel. While in some ways alarming, the Mall is not unique in this respect; U.S. police departments are turning to Israel with increasing regularity for tactical guidance and the latest surveillance technology, despite (or, perhaps, because of) the country's long record as an occupying force.[39] While the Mall and other security experts deem RAM a success, shopper testimony and several accounts of racial discrimination suggest otherwise.[40] Bobbie Allen, a Black man, sued the Mall after he was questioned by security guards and Bloomington law enforcement in a food court for over half an hour. Allen's suspicious behavior was sitting alone at a table, writing in a notebook, and waiting for his lunch date to arrive.[41]

In addition to analog tactics of surveillance, the Mall of America has likewise latched on to state-of-the-art technology that blurs the lines between marketing and policing. A team assigned to the "Enhanced Service Portal" follows social media posts mentioning the Mall and regularly responds to shoppers' posts.[42] Even without directly mentioning the Mall, software by Geofeedia allows the Mall's social media team to follow Instagram, Twitter, and Facebook posts made within geographic proximity of it. Together, this strategy allows the creation of the Mall's own online presence, almost instantaneously responding to user posts, thereby altering and extending its panoptic gaze into cyber space. According to the Mall's social media strategist, "We've had people say, 'Oh that's really creepy and cool that they saw my message. How did you see my message?'"[43]

Meanwhile, Geofeedia became a prominent player in policing Black Lives Matter protests. The company was the target of widely publicized critique by the American Civil Liberties Union for its role in working with police in tracking BLM protesters across the country.[44] The ACLU found that Geofeedia emailed an inquiry to the San Diego sheriff's office in 2014, noting that their software could be useful in tracking antipolice protesters.

Before it received such negative attention, Geofeedia boasted that it was a boon for retailers by aggregating Facebook, Instagram, and Twitter posts based on geographic location. In a demonstration video, which has since been removed from Geofeedia's website, the company details its relationship with the Mall of America. Not only could Geofeedia aggregate patrons' posts,[45] but in one highlighted instance, the software was able to detect an employee of Nickelodeon Universe, the Mall's amusement park, posting a picture of himself on Instagram smoking marijuana before work. Although the post did not mention the Mall or Nickelodeon Universe by name, Geofeedia aggregates all posts within a certain geographic proximity of the mall. Plus, the narrator points out, one can see the user's employee shirt in the photo.

Although the narrator did not specify how the mall then intervened in the situation, Geofeedia says elsewhere that "the team works with the local police department when necessary, providing them with social media content that assist with preventing or investigating crimes."[46] Conveniently for Geofeedia, an outpost of the Bloomington Police Department sits on the second floor of the mall itself. It should come as little surprise that the Nickelodeon Universe employee was a young Black man. We do not know if that employee was fired, arrested, or otherwise disciplined. We also do not know if that employee or employees like him, who might have worked on the days of the BLM protests, could have been included in Geofeedia's sweeping of potential protesters.

Using software to monitor protests at the mall isn't entirely new, either. The investigative reporting outlet *The Intercept* indicates the mall relied on various monitoring platforms—including Topsy, Monitor, and Kurrently—to keep tabs on Idle No More protests by Indigenous activists in 2012. This early practice with digital surveillance would come to serve mall officials well a few years later when the Black Lives Matter protests would target the shopping space during one of its busiest shopping weekends of the year.

By December 2014, Ferguson, Missouri, had erupted over the killing of Michael Brown, and protests reverberated across the country with news of subsequent injustices, including the non-indictment of Daniel Pantaleo for killing Eric Garner, announced on December 3. Over 2,000 protesters flocked to the Mall of America on December 20, 2014, filling the main rotunda and reclaiming the space as almost a public square.[47] "Join us at the Mall of America in solidarity with #BlackLivesMatter. It will surely be a #BlackChristmas," the Facebook event page read. Organizers warned protesters to prepare for heavy security, to refrain from bringing signs, and to fit in with the mall patrons. After circulating a call via text loop, protesters who had already entered the mall congregated around the Christmas tree. Trained marshals guarded the periphery of the rotunda for the short duration of the formal event, and upon ending, the crowd did not immediately disperse, but instead spilled out across the mall's winding hallways and throughout the three shopping floors where they chanted, staged die-ins, and confronted police.

Of the seven people I spoke to who attended this event, most reiterated the intent to "disrupt business as usual." Accounts like Cassandra's or Gabe's were common:

Cassandra: I'm kind of using one of the lines, but, like, there won't be any more business as usual, you know, if this is what's happening to our Black neighbors. You know that people get shot. So, like, sorry, your shop's gonna be closed for a couple hours. . . .

Gabe: I think part of the purpose of most protests is to disrupt the status quo and what I saw as a main influence was to trouble people's very comfortable sensibilities about how they live their lives and go about their everyday mundane activities in terms of like, um, shopping, eating, whatever activities they may do at the mall.

In this sense, as Gabe notes, this protest could have taken place at nearly any other location, to similar effect. At other times, the "business" in "business as usual" took on a different meaning, one tied more directly to capitalism, commerce, and policing:

Javier: There was a targeting and honing of specific economic sites and workplace sites. So come fall 2014, what had been like the pinnacle of occupying public space within a couple of weeks, people very rapidly . . . were taking over highways and bridges and tunnels and swarming places that were symbolic or otherwise centers of commerce.

Lori: One thing that I took away from it, from the consumerist culture of it too, was kind of harsh. So disrupting something that's consumerist when there's that big tag that oh it's all about family, but it's also about things. And kinda bringing that there are people that are missing out on their family that will never get them back, so doing it in a large public space that engages that consumeristic culture was also I believe a big part of it.

Gabe: [I] was really excited about this site for this particular rally slash protest, um, in thinking about the links between capitalism and racism. And what is, like, racial capitalism.

Racial capitalism, coined by Cedric Robinson, refers to how capitalism operates through perceived racial difference, in which value is produced through the exploitation of those differences.[48] One organizer, who was subsequently banned from the mall, told reporters, "When you disrupt the flow of capital . . . they actually start paying attention. That's the only way that they'll hear us."[49]

In swarming the Mall of America, Black Lives Matter protesters were simultaneously reclaiming what supposedly operates as a public square, while disrupting a symbol of technoprecarity and racial capitalism. A colleague of mine who attended this action added: "There is a direct line between their wealth and Black and Indigenous dispossession, debt, and death. So, when people mobilize to shine a light on the extraction and exploitation of life and labor, they are also demanding that these corporations come up off their wealth and come up off the land."

The spectacle was made all the more dramatic by the police, who projected the following message on a jumbotron: "This demonstration is not authorized and is in clear violation of Mall of America policy. We expect all participants to disperse at this time. Those who continue to demonstrate will be subject to arrest." (see figure 5.1). One participant, Lori, reflected:

Figure 5.1
Black Lives Matter protest at the Mall of America. *Source:* CC/Flickr/Nicholas Upton.

Lori: It was pretty *1984*. It was really creepy. They continued to display the screen that said, like, this is an unauthorized protest and you'll be asked to leave and trespassing and blah blah.

M: Can you say a little more about that and what that felt like? Or why that reference?

Lori: Just to have an autonomous voice coming down from above saying that you're not authorized to gather there was, it was creepy for one. But it was also . . . weird because it felt like your rights were being stripped of you. Because this place has such a perception of being a public space. Our tax dollars go towards it.

Similarly, Joey, a friend of mine, told me, "The disruption wasn't just of the space-time of the stores but also of people's subjective dispositions as consumers—both at the protest and through circulation of images of the protest—for example, highlighting the *1984* dystopian character of the giant TV screen telling people to leave." Gabe noted that through one of common chants he heard that day—"Who do you protect? Who do you serve?"—it became clear that the police operated as an apparatus not only of the state but also of capital and its many manifestations.

Tensions percolated as some organizers and attendees were targeted after the protest ended. Days later, Black Lives Matter Minneapolis posted on the event page: "City of Bloomington attorney Sandra Johnson says she will seek restitution for 'loss of profits' and police resources from young people of color she claims to identify as organizers." As a close reader of this manuscript pointed out, there's a lot to unpack with the term "profits." Beyond monetary meanings, profits might also refer to the benefits that come along with a diverse, welcoming, and inclusive brand image. The protests fundamentally challenged this idea, instead showing how these profits—in their various forms—are built on exploitation, violence, and dispossession. The Mall of America could not exist without the dispossession of Native land, the exploitation of working-class people, and the exclusion of any shopper deemed a "threat" to its image of family-friendly consumption.

Mall officials relied heavily on social media to track activists, as they did with the Idle No More movement. This time, they created a false Facebook account, friending key organizers, liking pages of local protest groups, and creating dossiers of at least ten people.[50] The Mall pressed charges against seventeen organizers, although a judge dismissed several charges—including aiding and abetting trespass, aiding and abetting unlawful assembly, and aiding and abetting disorderly conduct.[51] Meanwhile, charges were not dropped for thirty-six others who were not identified as key organizers.[52]

Media scholar John Fiske writes, "Shopping malls are where the strategy of the powerful is most vulnerable to tactical raids of the weak."[53] This claim remains true more than two decades later, even as technology has transformed the landscape of struggle. While in many ways serving the interests of capital and the state, these changes may allow new opportunities for rebellious alliances.

Toward a Critical Data Praxis

The Retail Action Project and Movement for Black Lives, making unique demands and employing distinct tactics, shared much in common. They both included, organized with, and advocated in the interest of precarious people on the margins of the economy and who are targets of the police state. Both movements politicized retail spaces, from the National Retail Federation to the Mall of America. While technology was not a central frame of either group's engagement with retail, it's clear that digital technologies, most notably big data and biometric surveillance, shaped the field within which these groups operated and point toward potential opportunities for future alliance.

If the concept of "technoprecarity" helps trace the digital characteristics of contemporary inequality, then feminist and critical data theorists put forward concepts to envision more just horizons. Rather than simply asking tech companies to grant their users privacy, feminist scholars and activists work toward a more anticapitalist and anti-state critique of surveillance. Many marginalized groups already live under watchful eye of the state—including poor single mothers, incarcerated people and their families, and Native communities—and no privacy setting is going to change that.[54]

Arun Kundnani remarked at the 2018 Subverting Surveillance Conference that "the antagonism of surveillance is not privacy, but the making of communities in struggle." Sociologists Simone Browne and Ruha Benjamin have terms to help describe the characteristics of these struggles, including "critical biometric consciousness" and "abolitionist consciousness."[55] These ideas helped me think about how what connects RAP and BLM is not only geography—in that they both protest in and around retail spaces—or demography—in that they both organize precarious people of color communities—but their visions of a better society: they are both building toward a *critical data praxis*. (Praxis means putting theory into action.) In other words, these groups collectively mobilize against the harms exacerbated by digital technology.

In a world in which digital technology blurs the lines between management, marketing, and surveillance, the development of critical data praxis is crucial. RAP, BLM, and other groups at the intersections of low-wage work, surveillance, and policing demand not just privacy, but justice.

Conclusion: Refashioning the Future of Work

Reflecting on what I've learned from this project, I think about two different questions. First: What can fast-fashion retail teach us about "the future of work"? Second, how can people who read this book take action?

Under this umbrella of "the future of work" usually sit debates about how digital technologies and automation will change the labor processes and the shape of the global workforce. In an afterword to the 2003 edition of *The Managed Heart,* Hochschild observes that "large parts of the 'emotional proletariat' are being automated out."[1] She says that while some jobs are being eliminated, other jobs in the care sector—including among childcare and healthcare workers—continue to grow. My foray into fast fashion presents a different picture.

What I found in fast fashion was not simply about the elimination of jobs by computers, but rather a transformation of work and life for people in fast-fashion retail. These workers are socialized into a world of on-demand labor and total flexibility well before being hired (chapter 1); their labor has become even further removed from interactive service work in the era of the *automated heart* (chapter 2); and their affective experiences of insecurity are compounded through digital surveillance and result in an *emotional labor of surveillance* (chapter 3). At the same time, fast fashion is also an industry whose labor struggles and entanglement with surveillance and policing across society may reveal avenues for creating more just worlds through *critical data praxis* (chapter 4).

In 2016, the White House released a report on automation and the future of work, saying that interactive occupations are least likely to face elimination due to automation. In their report, former President Obama's chief economics and technology advisors discuss the example of bus driving: while the actual driving of the bus might be automated by self-driving vehicles, school buses may still require a paid employee to watch over the riders. This interactive, emotional work can't be automated, the report implies. And yet, in fast fashion, it's precisely the interactive element of the job that's been taken over by computers. In other words, automation does not always take on rote tasks and leave humans to do the more creative—seemingly more human—work. In many ways, the implementation of these technologies removes creativity from existing roles, leaving little left *but* rote tasks.

Hochschild did, in fact, warn of these changes. In *The Managed Heart,* she wrote that if "automation and the decline of unskilled labor leads to a decline in emotional labor, as machines replace the personal delivery of services, then this general social track may come to be replaced by another that trains people to be controlled in more impersonal ways."[2] Where worker's hearts were once managed, today, many have been automated. The labor of interactive service work has almost disappeared, ostensibly because companies think their algorithms can know and serve customers better than human workers. These days, the work left to be done inside the stores resembles something close to a factory or fulfillment center. Similar trends have been noted at Amazon warehouses: it's humans, not robots, who perform the mind-numbing and physically exhausting labor of constantly picking and sorting items.[3] Technology has certainly not freed us from work, and it hasn't even left workers to focus on what is supposedly "uniquely human" about us: our ability to connect with, empathize with, and engage with other living beings.

As I found, being "controlled in more impersonal ways" includes automated scheduling and pervasive digital surveillance. I'm reminded of the rapper/singer/songwriter M.I.A.'s 2010 song "The Message." The song's lyrics trace the relationship between cell phones, the internet, and government surveillance. Upon its release, music critics deemed the song a "horribly paranoid rant." After the National Security Agency WikiLeaks confirmed the U.S. government was indeed collecting personal information on millions of people, music critics admitted M.I.A.'s song had been "more prescient than it seemed."[4] In a strange turn of events, six years later, in 2016, M.I.A. released a song in cooperation with fast-fashion giant H&M called "Rewear It" to encourage shoppers to recycle their clothes. I'd like to think that if M.I.A. knew that retailers were themselves entangled in this surveillance assemblage, she might have changed her tune.

I suspect that the digital technologies I examined in this book will become more commonplace across a range of occupations in coming years. As these phenomena become more well-known, I also suspect that efforts to counteract them will likewise proliferate. My time spent in labor movement and social movement spaces—as well as repeatedly dog-earing my copy of Kathi Weeks's book *The Problem with Work*[5] and revisiting Robin D. G. Kelley's article "'We Are Not What We Seem': Rethinking Black Working-Class Opposition in the Jim Crow South"[6]—encourages me to think about not only the "future *of* work" but also "futures *against* work." By that I mean that refashioning the future of work might mean working together to create alternative futures, against the harms of waged labor in the digital age.

Recent legislative actions, including in California and New York City, have attempted to make retail work more stable and predictable, including passing minimum wage increases to fifteen dollars per hour, ending on-call scheduling, and requiring employers to post schedules at least two weeks in advance.[7] Future research might thus look to California's and New York City's actions as a natural experiment of sorts, an opportunity to investigate how legislation that bans on-call scheduling and raises the minimum wage may change how retailers engage with employee monitoring technologies, and the extent to which these policy changes impact entry-level workers' health and well-being.

Some, like the head of the Retail Action Project, Rachel Laforest, see significance in these measures, as she mentioned in an interview with me:

> Banning on-call, you know, protects retail workers in a far better way than any software was going to. It protects retail workers' pockets in terms of hours. It protects their ability to care for family members. It protects their ability to go to school and figure out what their next steps, either inside or outside of the retail industry, look like. And those are not tied to the company's bottom line, but real quality of life issues or questions that had to be dealt with.

In other words, legislative actions might hold more leverage than technocratic solutions alone in engendering positive social change.

Creating futures against work should include using critical data praxis to produce fuller understandings of how data travels across institutional contexts. This approach would encourage labor movements to focus on how digital technology deepens insecurity and reinforces difference. With this lens, labor campaigns might mobilize young workers who are already tuned in to issues of police brutality and digital surveillance beyond the workplace. Economic and racial justice groups might draw on their shared histories, resources, and collective capacities to resist the growing phenomenon of facial recognition software, increasingly common in both retail and public settings.[8] Conceivably, racial justice organizers might also collaborate with labor organizers in challenging, repurposing, or abolishing digital management platforms like Kronos, which not only produce automated flexible scheduling software and biometric fingerprint scanners that I described in previous chapters, but also are geared toward law enforcement to aid in "episodes of civil unrest, when a large-scale disruption requires rapid deployment of additional officers, including those with specialized training."[9] Keeping our analyses centered on tech as an amplifier of current inequalities will promote collective and interconnected struggles for liberation.

In considering these futures against work, romanticizing digital technologies risks sidelining nondigital modes of suffering, surveillance, and resilience. Just as how earlier in the book retail worker Ryan highlighted the prevalence of old-school pat-downs of employees, we must remember that not all surveillance is high-tech. Digital defense and digital organizing should thus be only one component of a broader arsenal spanning the high- and low-tech divide. Part of the "critical" in critical data praxis requires holding these tensions. Only then will we be able to understand, interrogate, and confront how digital technology shapes everyday life, from our devices to our jobs to our streets.

The second and related question—how might people who read this book take action?—is in some ways thornier for me to answer. When I present on my research, I am often met with eager questions about alternatives to fast fashion, including "slow" or "zero waste" clothing, which might have fewer disastrous consequences on the environment or workers. But we must proceed with caution. Even secondhand clothing comes with its own fallout; thrift store CEOs take home huge salaries while exploiting workers who are disabled, sending only a small fraction of proceeds to charity, and dumping unwanted garments on poor communities the world over.[10]

We should be especially wary of just-in-time retail's attempts to rebrand itself. While working at Style Queen, for instance, they promoted their "green" clothing line, called "Aware." During one of our morning meetings, our manager proposed a workplace lunch to boost morale. We had been feeling down after he told us the company had eliminated our already meager bonuses. This lunch, however, would be a potluck, since the company was attempting to be cost- "Aware," he clarified with a grin and a wink. I was stunned. By conflating *ecologically* friendly practices with ones that are *economically* friendly, the manager recoded "Aware"-ness to convince me and my underpaid coworkers that our exploitative workplace conditions were in the pursuit of ostensibly progressive goals. It seems greenwashing can be used to mask ongoing worker exploitation as well as ongoing damage to the planet.

Perhaps more promising than ethical consumption are calls for radical design or design justice.[11] While the term "design" often connotes the creation of tools and products, many critical design scholars consider how in designing *things* we are also *designing worlds*. Might we design clothing in a way that creates new, more liberatory futures? In her book *Race after Technology*, Ruha Benjamin talks about the Hyphen-Labs, "an international team of women of color who work at the intersection of technology, art, science, and futurism," whose designs include "earrings for recording police altercations, and visors and other clothing that prevent facial recognition."[12] Sometimes, friends will ask me if I know of companies where they can buy clothes that are eco-friendly and ethically produced. Projects like Hyphen-Labs challenge us to think about not only how to *omit* cruelty from the design and production process but how to use clothing as a *tool against* the cruelties of digital precarity.

Part of my struggle to answer the question of how people who read this book might take action is that academia trained me to spot shortcomings in potential solutions. I entered graduate school with an *either/or* framework of change. Mainstream solutions were bad, but "radical" solutions were good. The longer I spent in school, the more I developed a *neither/nor* framework: no solution was good enough; every effort to create positive social change, no matter how critical or radical, held a dark counterrevolutionary lining waiting to be discovered. Scholars who pointed out those flaws were celebrated, awarded, and promoted. Often, people who practiced these ways of thinking rarely put forward alternatives. I found this framework commonly perpetuated in left organizing circles as well. In me, it led to hopelessness and burnout. Why try to do anything if everything is flawed?

More recently, I have been attempting to embrace a *both/and* perspective. Put simply, let's try everything. Let's do anything we can from where we're at, if we know we aren't directly strengthening the thing we are attempting to work against. That could include putting the brakes on constant consumption, holding clothing swaps with our friends, setting up or supporting neighborhood free stores where people leave what they don't want and people take what they do, washing the clothes of our unhoused neighbors, boycotting especially harmful brands, writing to our elected officials, supporting prison worker strikes (especially where labor is performed for giant retail corporations), starting a reading group about confronting surveillance (the "Digital Defense Playbook" by Our Data Bodies is a good place to start),[13] talking to our coworkers about what they know about worker surveillance, collectively refusing to work to get our demands met, doing die-ins at all the malls, enlisting the support of the press and labor unions and labor lawyers, and supporting international labor organizing across the retail supply chains. Together, we can create new threads. Together, we can fashion futures against work.

Afterword

On May 26, 2020, I sat at my desk in Minneapolis to review my field notes. I had just finished the semester teaching at a community college, and I needed to get in the proper headspace before I could write this book in earnest. I couldn't believe it had already been over five years since I began the project. And yet, as I read, I was overwhelmed not by how much had changed but by how much had remained the same. I revisited marching on the one-year anniversary of Eric Garner's death and witnessing die-ins in front of the world's largest H&M in Herald Square in New York City. I took a short break as I closed one file and opened the next. My partner walked into the room and told me the news; video of the Minneapolis Police killing a Black man was circulating. Following the murders of Jamar Clark in 2015 and Philando Castille in 2016—not to mention many others across the United States—it felt like S.O.S.: the same old shit. I messaged my friends to meet up at the protest planned for that evening at Chicago Avenue and 38th Street—outside Cup Foods, the site of George Floyd's murder. I didn't get much work done that day.

Later, I marched with hundreds of people from Cup Foods to the Minneapolis 3rd Police Precinct about three miles away. I stood in the intersection, observing the multiracial crowd. Young people stood defiantly atop a structure near the precinct, holding a spray-painted banner reading "I can't breathe" and "Another Black Man!" A group of Native residents waved an American Indian Movement flag from the other end of the crowd. Two young white men walked by with "FTP" (Fuck the Police) scrawled in marker on the back of their T-shirts. I ran into a friend of mine who had written "ACAB" (All Cops Are Bastards) across her COVID-19 face mask. The skies opened and rain began to fall.

I walked a few blocks home to eat. I shoveled leftovers into my mouth while I checked Twitter. In the minutes after I had left—or perhaps even while I was still there—protesters egged and smashed windows of police cruisers. The police department soon fired back with flash grenades and tear gas. The protesters showed little sign of stopping.

Police pushed the remaining crowd across Lake Street to the Target parking lot where the protesters eventually barricaded themselves with stacks of red shopping carts. Once again, a mega just-in-time retailer became a site of righteous outrage against a brutal murder at the hands of police. S.O.S. indeed. I listened to the sounds of heavy rain and rounds of "less lethal" weapons popping well into the night.

The next afternoon, I woke from a nap to the sounds of helicopters buzzing overhead. My partner was gone. "Where r u?" I texted him. "At the police station," he replied. We lived just a few blocks away. "Is something going down?" He responded with a photo of a crowd facing the precinct with their hands in the air. Three officers stood on the roof. One had his weapon aimed at the crowd below.

A friend and I headed back to the scene that evening before sunset. Even more officers flanked the roof and the precinct perimeter, sporadically firing tear gas and rubber bullets into the streets. Roaming the blocks surrounding the intersection, we witnessed the liquor store being looted and graffitied, people smashing the windows to a check-cashing place amid cheers, others seeking protection behind a barricade of Target shopping carts, and young people hanging out the windows of graffiti-covered cars. The mood felt as varied as the people in the streets. There was rage, mourning, celebration, fear, and cooperation, all at once.

We headed to the bustling Target parking lot, which was seemingly devoid of law enforcement. Vehicles joyfully rolled through. Throngs of people entered the store's back door while even more came out the front with their arms full. I looked around to take it all in; I noticed two rainbows hugging the sky. Someone had

Target, Lake St. *Source:* CC/Flickr/Lori Schaull.

spray painted near the store entrance: "everything for everybody."

If my ethnographic research taught me that many contemporary retailers rely on technologies originally crafted for law enforcement, Target flipped that script by developing technologies later utilized by police. Following the abovementioned Minneapolis Uprising, Target Workers Unite—an independent initiative run by rank-and-file workers—tweeted a series of news stories about Target's role in high-tech surveillance and policing. In 2011, Target had told Minnesota Public Radio News that it allowed Minneapolis police to access its "forensics crime lab" free of charge.[1] On top of that, Target Corporation worked with the Minneapolis Police Department and donated $300,000 to develop the SafeZone

Collaborative, which created an extensive network of video camera surveillance across downtown Minneapolis.[2] The company rolled out similar initiatives in cities across the country.

In the months that followed the uprising, Minneapolis, as well as communities around the United States, took the prospect of defunding and abolishing police more seriously than ever in recent history. Target's role as an innovator in surveillance tools should encourage us to consider retail corporations as a potential site of struggle beyond the abolitionist horizon. Without police, will Target, Amazon, Walmart, Zara, H&M, and other major retailers step in as cities' new security?

The Minneapolis Uprising—known also as the George Floyd Rebellion—brewed within the context of the COVID-19 pandemic, which created another opportunity for corporations to build their worker-monitoring muscles. A few days after the infamous burning of the Minneapolis police's 3rd Precinct, along with widespread fires and looting across the city, I checked in via email with some of my community college students who worked at nearby Target locations. In earlier conversations, they told me about the lack of personal protective equipment as COVID-19 hit and the difficulties of maintaining social distance in cramped shopping aisles. One student emailed me back: "Thanks for checking in. I'm doing well. Very mentally burned out though, having worked through COVID and now looting threats." This students' comments reminded me of my student in New York City, described at the beginning of this book, who expressed similar sentiments (minus COVID) several years prior. In this case, Target was directly involved in the exploitation and slow death of its workers amid the pandemic, and potentially implicated in extrajudicial killings of surrounding community members by developing technology used by law enforcement.

As I write this afterword, the United States has been suffering from the COVID-19 pandemic for two years. While many white-collar workers labor from home, retail workers who are still employed have not had that luxury.[3]

Earlier in the pandemic, sometime during the summer of 2020, I went to the Mall of America, mostly out of curiosity. It did not feel much less crowded than usual. I felt frustration and anger simmer at the roughly one out of ten people not wearing face masks. Evidence of the disproportionate impact of COVID on poor communities, Indigenous communities, and communities of color abounds.

Meanwhile, the world of online shopping has exploded, and so too have accounts of worker exploitation. With far fewer brick-and-mortar stores, we see retail workers' struggles ongoing at the point of production, including among garment workers in Myanmar, who have been leading militant strikes and pro-democracy protests.[4] In March 2021, H&M paused placing orders with its forty-five Myanmar-based suppliers.[5] Workers' struggles aren't limited to the garment workers, either. We also see them behind the curtain of the white-collar retail tech companies, where multiple employees have committed suicide in the face of intense pressure.[6] And in between the factory floors and corporate offices are the same kinds of workers I describe throughout this book who continue to sell in person.

Across Amazon distribution centers and among the few remaining brick-and-mortar stores, new technologies have emerged to track the spread of the coronavirus among "essential" workers. Although these tools aim to protect the people who must be out in public to receive their paychecks, critics say these technologies can potentially violate workers' privacy.[7] Because there are so few laws about worker surveillance, and because these tools purport to do good, there is even less oversight than usual. When and if this pandemic ends, we may very well see a new precedent of ever-more-limitless worker monitoring.

The good news is that we are living through a high moment of struggle, meaning workers, activists, and everyday people are regularly coming together to create change. Amazon workers in Bessemer, Alabama, attempted to unionize through the Retail, Wholesale and Department Store Union,[8] the same union that the Retail Action Project was created out of (chapter 4). Recognizing the difficulty of formal unionization in this historical moment, the Teamsters are organizing Amazon warehouse workers and delivery drivers in Iowa to push for higher wages and less stringent productivity requirements.[9] Across the board, retails' app-mediated workers—including those who deliver goods through Target's app, Shipt[10]—are organizing to improve their work conditions.

I hope that this book inspires more agitation, movement, and organizing across the global supply chain.[11]

Appendix: Researching Retail

Between 2015 and 2017, I conducted workplace ethnography at two of the nation's largest fast-fashion stores near Times Square in New York City. *Ethnography* is a research method utilized by anthropologists and sociologists that entails immersing oneself in a social context in order to understand it in depth. Usually, ethnographers will keep a diary of sorts—called field notes—describing every aspect of the social world they witness and participate in. The idea is that this kind of research provides richer insight than what one could get from surveys or interviews alone; it allows researchers to "see and understand power relations being made and unfolding in real time."[1] Some ethnographers believe, for example, that self-reported data that respondents provide in surveys or interviews leads to omission of the taken-for-granted aspects of everyday life. In my case, I relied on *participant ethnography*. I wanted to understand more about retail labor, so instead of just interviewing workers or observing them as a shopper (though I also did both things), I became employed in fast-fashion retail myself.

Because ethnography is conducted in "the real world," I encountered many challenges and ethical dilemmas along the way.

My first dilemma arose during the planning stages. Like all academic ethnographers, I collaborated with my university's Institutional Review Board (IRB) in this process. The IRB is a committee that is supposed to help ensure that any research conducted by people affiliated with the university involving human subjects is done ethically. (My friend and colleague Mingwei Huang has written about how this process can go wrong. For example, prioritizing the well-being of the research subjects can sometimes neglect the well-being of the researchers.[2]) The IRB suggested that I go undercover—what academics call *covert*—for the ethnographic portion of the project. I was a bit surprised when they suggested this, since it's rare for sociologists to conduct research covertly. One of central tenets of human subject research is that people involved in the project must consent to participating in the project and they must be able to opt out of the study at any time. If I didn't tell anyone I was conducting this research, it would be impossible for them to consent, and thus seemed to be a blatant misuse of my power.

However, as the IRB pointed out, in this case, fast-fashion retailers would have been unlikely to hire me at all if I were forthcoming about my project. On top of that, my coworkers might have faced negative ramifications from employers if they became associated with my research. For example, I considered not telling my employer about my research but letting in a few trusted coworkers. This strategy could have helped me build deeper relationships with my colleagues. Yet if my employer were to discover my research intentions and disapprove of them, my coworkers who knew about the project could have been fired or otherwise disciplined. And if my coworkers didn't want to be involved, there was no way for me to un-tell them about the project. So, to avoid adding extra risk to my coworkers' already stressful and unstable jobs, I remained covert to both my employers and my colleagues.

During the summer of 2015, I became employed as an entry-level sales associate at McFashion and took rigorous field notes on my experiences working in the store, typing notes into my cellphone during lunch breaks and commutes home and elaborating on those notes at night or the next day. By participating in and observing the application and hiring processes, new employee orientation and training, and work processes, I gained an intimate sense of daily life in the fast-fashion industry.

I quit my job at McFashion in August to focus on my work as a teaching assistant. After all, I knew McFashion would not allow me to hold a second job. The following spring of 2016, I reentered the retail job market. I was teaching asynchronous courses online, which allowed me to offer "open availability" to prospective employers, and I thought I would get hired quickly. It took me several months to finally land this second job, and because of that I felt like a failure. And even more immediately worrying, I wasn't sure I'd be able to pay my all my bills without a job. On March 23, 2016, I wrote in my field notes:

> I woke up today super anxious. I'm freaking out about money. The class I'm teaching was only 8 weeks, so it just wrapped up. I have money to cover my rent and MetroCard for April and May, but I still need money to cover my student loans ($200/mo), phone bill ($50/mo), and food. Plus, I have to pay in for my freelance editing taxes (~$200). I think I can scrape by for the next few months, but I have no idea how I'll make it through the summer. I should see if I can get food stamps or defer my student loans, even though I don't think I qualify as a full-time student this semester [I wanted to avoid paying student fees, so I figured the money would be better put toward paying off loans]. . . . I got a call Tuesday evening from Style Queen, which felt good. I got an interview scheduled, but not until April 8. Anxiety set in again.

I felt as if my fieldwork was at a standstill. Only later did I realize that those periods of uncertainty amid job seeking were also part of my research. Indeed, much of this experience informed what is now chapter 2 of this book.

After several call-backs and interviews with multiple companies, I finally landed a job with another retailer, Style Queen. With this second position, I hoped to gain employment in the stocking department, allowing me to explicate the different components of the labor process more fully. Although I was again hired as a sales associate, this store trained workers "globally"; that is, all entry-level employees worked in the stockroom, on the sales floor, in the fitting room, and at the cash register. This also meant that my schedule fluctuated even more dramatically at Style Queen, since people who worked in the back room had to start as early as 6 a.m. Some days I would wake up as early as 4:30 a.m. but could be working as late as 11 p.m. that night. My sleep, and my mental health, suffered.

In documenting my experiences working in these stores, I made a point to record details that seemed to exceed the labor process, which I experienced outside the physical and temporal boundaries of waged work. For example, I took note of how I had to "hurry up and wait" to catch the A train to Midtown in time for my shift, the standing-room-only rush-hour subway rides, the glowing fluorescent lights and pulsing store soundtrack that gave me migraines so bad I vomited after one shift, the long walks to and from the subway (I was mugged on my way to catch the 4:50 a.m. train for my 6 a.m. shift, an experience that my sympathetic coworkers could relate to), and the anxiety of trying to pay rent in New York City on such scrappy pay. Indeed, many of these experiences are common to public transit commuters and members of the urban working class. When I worked in fast fashion, I was not merely a researcher attempting to gain an insider's perspective on low-wage labor; I was also a graduate student with no safety net. I was privileged to receive $5,000 supplemental funding from my graduate program during the spring of 2016. In my writing, I attempt to remain aware of both the distinctions and points of overlap between my coworkers and myself.

Especially given that I conducted my observations covertly, I took several steps to ensure my colleagues' privacy remains protected. I have given pseudonyms to my coworkers and changed identifying information of my employers—which I here have called McFashion and Style Queen. In my ethnographic observations, my primary subject was not my coworkers but rather my employers. My field notes focused less on the intimate details of the people I worked with and more on the labor process and my personal experiences working at each location. Protecting my colleagues' privacy is one reason why I remained a relatively short time in each field site. I felt that in each location I was able to reach sufficient saturation in terms of my understandings of the labor process and lived experiences of being employed by each company, while avoiding close relationships with my coworkers. Especially at Style Queen, opportunities arose to socialize with my coworkers outside the workplace, and while I would occasionally walk with them to the train and chat during lunch breaks, I refrained from pursuing time with them beyond that.

One aspect of retail work that I gained knowledge of, and which I share some aspects of in this book, are the various ways that workers attempt to evade or resist surveillance. These practices exist within the centuries-long tradition of workers' struggles.[3] Hearing about and witnessing such modes of resistance excited me and brought a liveliness to what was an otherwise miserable work experience. Quite simply, I want to write about things that inspired me and helped me envision and work toward a better world.

I have been rightly challenged by some of my colleagues to be careful about what information I share. Many of these warnings relate to critiques of Alice Goffman's book, *On the Run: Fugitive Life in an American City*, which describes how Black communities in Philadelphia evade daily police surveillance across the urban landscape. While receiving enormous praise from some scholars, others criticized Goffman for making subaltern methods of survival known to the public. A generous reading might say Goffman's book and others like it are written for the purpose of highlighting and attempting to ameliorate inequality. Yet, especially when written by someone with such enormous privilege—Goffman is the daughter of famed sociological theorist Erving Goffman—books like Goffman's can in fact exacerbate the harms they supposedly critique.[4] For example, if and when criminologists and law enforcement read her accounts of how poor Black people avoid being tracked by police, the state may very well revise its tactics to more efficiently and thoroughly monitor these communities.

The debates around Goffman's book encouraged me to always keep in mind: For whom am I writing my book? Whom might it benefit and whom could it harm?

This book began as a dissertation that I wrote to satisfy my graduate school requirements and my PhD committee. In transforming the dissertation into a book, I had a broader audience in mind. Certainly, I hope this book will be read by other scholars of work, retail, technology, and social change. But beyond that, I hope this book gets into the hands of undergraduate students who might be working retail, or whatever iteration of it exists by the time this book hits the shelves. I hope such readers might find solace, a little clarity, and even some inspiration in what this book contains. I also wrote this book for my friends, many of whom have attempted to organize their own workplaces in some form and almost all of whom are as worried as I am about how technology will continue to make our lives and the lives of people we care about worse. Finally, I wrote this book for organizers and activists, who likely know far more than I do about most of the topics in this book. I hope this book might amplify their valiant efforts.

But I am not naive. I know that if in the wrong hands, this book could be used to inform further evolution of retail worker management and surveillance technologies. For that reason, I have chosen to alter some details of how my coworkers and interviewees evaded surveillance. Other examples I've omitted altogether. During my time in the field, I attempted to practice a political commitment to my coworkers. While on the clock, I prioritized assisting coworkers over most customers, covering them when they needed bathroom breaks, and giving away several of my shifts to my coworkers, whose requests for more hours—scrawled in pencil and pinned to the break-room bulletin board—consistently reminded me that they might benefit from the hours more than me. My political commitment to my coworkers also meant that I knew I wanted to dedicate a substantial portion of fieldwork to volunteering with organizations aiming to improve the conditions of retail labor. I return to this topic below.

To supplement my field notes, and to access personal stories and narratives that I wasn't able to obtain through covert participant ethnography, I conducted semi-structured interviews with twenty workers about their lives and experiences working in the industry. My experience as a retail employee informed the questions I asked. Since I had learned that automated schedulers, biometric fingerprint time clocks, and digital cash register systems were common tools that shaped employee experience, I asked open-ended questions about their experiences with each. While some interviewees I connected with through word of mouth, I recruited the vast majority online. Interviews generally lasted around one hour and covered life history, work experiences, and perceptions of the movement to raise the minimum wage and the Black Lives Matter movement. Most of the people I talked to were located in New York City, but a handful lived in other cities throughout the United States, and one lived in Canada. Among those who lived in other locations, some had worked in fast fashion in New York City, while others had not. I changed the names of everyone I interviewed.

As I reread my interview transcripts and field notes to identify key themes—a process qualitative researchers call "coding"—I noticed that what I heard from retail workers in other cities was similar to what I had heard in New York. And major themes were fairly similar across interviewees who worked for different companies. An interview with an executive director of a retail labor workers' center supports this finding. "If you stripped away the name of the company and you listened to two different workers talk," she told me, "you wouldn't know who's talking about who." In a sense, then, I attempt to generalize from my interviews and experiences the new dominant model for how people today shop and work in retail. However, companies based outside the United States (such as Zara, H&M, and Uniqlo) adhere to different labor laws in their home countries than those based domestically (such as Forever 21); these potential global differences could constitute a future research project.

For the most part, this book is anchored in a comparison of two cases—McFashion and Style Queen—to understand how digital worker management and surveillance operated across distinct sites. This comparative case study approach allowed me to identify themes that I encountered across sites—including general approaches to worker recruitment, central technologies employed to manage workers, and common worker grievances and resistance tactics—which were supported through my interviews with workers across the fast-fashion industry.

At the same time, my research involved constant movement and cross-pollination across people and locations. I informally shared my reflections of working at McFashion and Style Queen with RAP organizers; my volunteering with RAP—and, specifically, participation in an annual protest at the meeting of the National Retail Federation, which I describe in chapter 4—inspired additional fieldwork at retail industry conferences, which appears in chapter 3; my engagement with BLM infused my informal fieldwork interactions and formal interviews; many RAP organizers had themselves participated in BLM protests; and most BLM protesters I interviewed were at least aware of movements to raise the minimum wage, if not of RAP. My ethnography moved back and forth across the broader urban landscape, taking seriously the "fluid rather than solidly implanted"[5] nature of life and dissent in the twenty-first century.

More than any traditional sociological approach of integrating theory and method (such as grounded, abductive, or extended case methods), I found myself most inspired by an orientation to research that I never learned about in my graduate studies, called workers' inquiry.[6] This Marxist approach is rooted in the efforts of scholars and activists in the mid-twentieth century who attempted to use Marxist theory to engage in activist research. This orientation attempts to understand the conditions of labor based on the experiences and testimonies of workers, not solely for the sake of knowledge production, but rather with an eye toward mapping opportunities for worker organizing and creating structural change. Multiple factions debated questions such as who constitutes the working class and whether sociology can ever truly pave a path toward liberation. This book does not draw a line in the sand with those debates, but readers might notice how the book is informed by similar questions, including in considering who constitutes the technoprecariat and striving to create scholarship that contributes to a critical data praxis (explored in chapter 4).

Throughout the duration of my fieldwork, I also volunteered with the Retail Action Project, a retail workers' advocacy group, which I discuss in more detail in chapter 4. I showed up for regular meetings and rallies, helped survey retail workers around the city, and phoned RAP members and contacts to remind them of upcoming events. For in-depth perspectives, I interviewed five RAP organizers with whom I worked closely (and to whom I gave pseudonyms), as well as the RAP director. These interviews covered their work histories (most RAP organizers were former retail workers) and perspectives on the retail labor movement.

Additionally, since my earliest encounters with fast-fashion workers—my students—pointed to connections with movements for racial justice, I took notes on Black Lives Matter protests I participated in during the course of my fieldwork. I interviewed seven BLM activists whom I recruited online, speaking specifically with those who had participated in protests in or around retail spaces. These interviews sought participants' recollections of certain actions and their perceptions of retail's relevance to Black Lives Matter, and vice versa.

Beyond that, I took special effort to examine the technologies used to track workers. Sociology has a long history of studying historically underinvested communities, but this often has the effect of pathologizing behaviors and blaming poverty on lack of work ethic or proper moral standing. While working Style Queen and McFashion, I paid attention to the obvious and less obvious ways my performance and behavior were monitored. I built on these findings by attending the loss prevention conference detailed in chapter 3; I discuss that experience in more depth in my chapter in the anthology *Captivating Technology*.[7] That research extended the scope of my inquiry from the fast-fashion retail workplace to the broader industries of digital surveillance and security that end up shaping workers' everyday lives. Future research could more explicitly *study up*, which is an ethnographic research method of immersing one's self in and attempting to understand institutions and networks of power (as opposed my approach to this book, which is primarily an account of fast fashion labor "from below," that is, from the perspective of primarily entry-level workers).[8] Such research might focus on how retail managers interface with digital technologies and make decisions based on data. Studying up might also investigate how data analysts, software engineers, and white-collar fast-fashion workers reproduce these systems of surveillance and control. Research that embeds itself in the elite networks of fast-fashion shareholders and C-suite executives could reveal how those in power talk about and attempt to shape the future of retail.

Notes

Introduction

1. Arne L. Kalleberg, *Good Jobs, Bad Jobs: The Rise of Polarized and Precarious Employment Systems in the United States, 1970s to 2000s* (New York: Russell Sage Foundation, 2011).

2. Alec MacGillis, *Fulfillment: Winning and Losing in One-Click America* (New York: Farrar, Straus and Giroux, 2021).

3. Alex Rosenblat, "The Truth about How Uber's App Manages Drivers," *Harvard Business Review*, April 6, 2016.

4. Mary L. Gray and Siddharth Suri, *Ghost Work: How to Stop Silicon Valley from Building a New Global Underclass* (Boston: Houghton Mifflin Harcourt, 2019).

5. "Bossware and Employment Tech Database," Coworker, November 17, 2021, https://home.coworker.org/worktech.

6. Edward P. Thompson, "Time, Work-Discipline, and Industrial Capitalism," *Past & Present*, no. 38 (1967): 93.

Chapter 1

1. Christopher Mele, "Macy's Will Cut 10,000 Jobs after Poor Holiday Sales," *New York Times*, January 4, 2017, http://www.nytimes.com/2017/01/04/business/macys-jobs-layoffs.html.

2. Hayley Peterson, "Warren Buffett Just Confirmed the Death of Retail as We Know It," *Business Insider*, May 8, 2017, http://www.businessinsider.com/warren-buffett-just-confirmed-the-death-of-retail-as-we-know-it-2017-5; Derek Thompson, "Death of the Salesmen: Technology's Threat to Retail Jobs," *The Atlantic*, June 2013, https://www.theatlantic.com/magazine/archive/2013/06/death-of-the-salesmen/309309; Derek Thompson, "The Sad, Slow Death of America's Retail Workforce," *The Atlantic*, April 15, 2014, https://www.theatlantic.com/business/archive/2014/04/the-sad-slow-death-of-americas-retail-workforce/360635/; Robin Wigglesworth, "Will the Death of US Retail Be the Next Big Short?," *Financial Times*, July 16, 2017, https://www.ft.com/content/d34ad3a6-5fd3-11e7-91a7-502f7ee26895.

3. Derek Thompson, "What in the World Is Causing the Retail Meltdown of 2017?," *The Atlantic*, April 10, 2017, https://www.theatlantic.com/business/archive/2017/04/retail-meltdown-of-2017/522384.

4. John Kell, "H&M Locations Are Popping Up All Over," Fortune.com, May 20, 2015, http://fortune.com/2015/05/20/hm-store-locations.

5. Alden Wicker, "Fast Fashion Is Creating an Environmental Crisis," *Newsweek*, September 1, 2016, http://www.newsweek.com/2016/09/09/old-clothes-fashion-waste-crisis-494824.html.

6. Forever 21, "About Us," accessed July 18, 2017, http://www.forever21.com/Company/About.aspx?br=f21.

7. H&M Group, "Markets," accessed July 18, 2017, http://about.hm.com/en/about-us/markets-and-expansion.html; Lois Weiss, "Inditex Buys $280M Soho Building for New Zara Store," *New York Post* (blog), January 8, 2015, http://nypost.com/2015/01/08/inditex-buys-280m-soho-building-for-new-zara-store.

8. FashionNetwork, "Target Pursues Fast Fashion with New Private Brands," FashionNetwork.com, August 22, 2017, https://us.fashionnetwork.com/news/target-pursues-fast-fashion-with-new-private-brands,859620.html.

9. Alina Selyukh, "Forever 21 Files for Bankruptcy, May Close up to 178 U.S. Stores," NPR.org, September 30, 2019, https://www.npr

.org/2019/09/30/765834556/forever-21-files-for-bankruptcy-may-close-up-to-178-u-s-stores.

10. Jonathan Crary, *24/7: Late Capitalism and the Ends of Sleep* (London: Verso, 2014).

11. Andrew Morgan, dir., *The True Cost* (Bullfrog Films, 2016).

12. Elizabeth L. Cline, *Overdressed: The Shockingly High Cost of Cheap Fashion* (New York: Penguin, 2012).

13. Terry Nguyen, "Fast Fashion, Explained," Vox, February 3, 2020, https://www.vox.com/the-goods/2020/2/3/21080364/fast-fashion-h-and-m-zara.

14. Kell, "H&M Locations Are Popping up All Over."

15. Felipe Caro and Victor Martínez-de-Albéniz, "Fast Fashion: Business Model Overview and Research Opportunities," in *Retail Supply Chain Management*, ed. Narendra Agrawal and Stephen A. Smith (New York: Springer US, 2015), 237–264.

16. Edna Bonacich and Jake Wilson, "Organizing Wal-Mart's Logistics Workers," *New Labor Forum* 14, no. 2 (July 1, 2005): 67–75.

17. Hiroko Tabuchi, "Retailers Feel the Heat of Lost Winter Clothing Sales," *New York Times*, December 15, 2015, http://www.nytimes.com/2015/12/16/business/retailers-feel-the-heat-of-lost-winter-clothing-sales.html.

18. Edna Bonacich and Richard Appelbaum, *Behind the Label: Inequality in the Los Angeles Apparel Industry* (Berkeley: University of California Press, 2000); Minh-Ha T. Pham, "The High Cost of High Fashion," *Jacobin*, June 13, 2017, http://jacobinmag.com/2017/06/fast-fashion-labor-prada-gucci-abuse-designer; Morgan, *The True Cost*; Juliet Schor and Karen Elizabeth White, *Plenitude: The New Economics of True Wealth* (New York: Penguin Press, 2010), http://www.denkwerkzukunft.de/downloads/Schor-ppt.pdf.

19. Bonacich and Appelbaum, *Behind the Label*; Almudena Carracedo, dir., *Made in L.A.* (2007) (film).

20. Shamima Akhter, "Endless Misery of Nimble Fingers: The Rana Plaza Disaster," *Asian Journal of Women's Studies* 20, no. 1 (2014): 137–147; Dina M. Siddiqi, "Starving for Justice: Bangladeshi Garment Workers in a 'Post-Rana Plaza' World," *International Labor and Working-Class History* 87 (2015): 165–173.

21. Jana Kasperkevic, "Rana Plaza Collapse: Workplace Dangers Persist Three Years Later, Reports Find," *The Guardian*, May 31, 2016, https://www.theguardian.com/business/2016/may/31/rana-plaza-bangladesh-collapse-fashion-working-conditions.

22. Marc Bain, "H&M, Gap, and Walmart Are Accused of Widespread Worker Abuse," Quartz, March 31, 2016, https://qz.com/695763/a-web-of-terror-insecurity-and-a-high-level-of-vulnerability-hm-gap-and-walmart-are-accused-of-hundreds-of-acts-of-worker-abuse; Prak Chan Thul, "Hundreds Sick in Mass Fainting at Cambodian Factory," Reuters, August 25, 2011, http://www.reuters.com/article/us-cambodia-faintings-idUSTRE77O2TC20110825.

23. "Cambodia Garment Workers Killed in Clashes with Police," *BBC News*, January 3, 2014, http://www.bbc.com/news/world-asia-25585054.

24. Associated Press, "Zara Workers Hiding Tags in Garments with Pleas for Wages," *New York Post* (blog), November 5, 2017, https://nypost.com/2017/11/05/zara-workers-hiding-tags-in-garments-with-pleas-for-wages.

25. Carracedo, *Made in L.A.*

26. Natalie Kitroeff, "Factories That Made Clothes for Forever 21, Ross Paid Workers $4 an Hour, Labor Department Says," *LA Times*, November 16, 2016, http://www.latimes.com/business/la-fi-wage-theft-forever-ross-20161116-story.html.

27. Nicola Davis, "Fast Fashion Speeding toward Environmental Disaster, Report Warns," *The Guardian*, April 7, 2020, https://www.theguardian.com/fashion/2020/apr/07/fast-fashion-speeding-toward-environmental-disaster-report-warns.

28. Emma Bowman and Sarah McCammon, "Can Fast Fashion and Sustainability Be Stitched Together?," NPR.org, July 27, 2019, https://

www.npr.org/2019/07/27/745418569/can-fast-fashion-and-sustain ability-be-stitched-together.

29. Luz Claudio, "Waste Couture: Environmental Impact of the Clothing Industry," *Environmental Health Perspectives* 115, no. 9 (2007): A448–A454; Ian Tucker, "The Five: Ways That Fashion Threatens the Planet," *The Guardian*, June 23, 2019, https://www .theguardian.com/fashion/2019/jun/23/five-ways-fashion-damages -the-planet.

30. Rachel Bick, Erika Halsey, and Christine C. Ekenga, "The Global Environmental Injustice of Fast Fashion," *Environmental Health* 17, no. 1 (December 27, 2018): 92.

31. OLEM US EPA, "Textiles: Material-Specific Data," Collections and Lists, US EPA, 2018, https://www.epa.gov/facts-and-figures-about -materials-waste-and-recycling/textiles-material-specific-data.

32. Bowman and McCammon, "Can Fast Fashion and Sustainability Be Stitched Together?"

33. Minh-Ha T. Pham, "A World without Sweatshops: Abolition Not Reform," SSRN Scholarly Paper (Rochester, NY: Social Science Research Network, June 4, 2021), https://papers.ssrn.com/abstract=3860253.

34. Susan Porter Benson, *Counter Cultures: Saleswomen, Managers, and Customers in American Department Stores, 1890–1940* (Urbana: University of Illinois Press, 1986).

35. Kjerstin Gruys, "Does This Make Me Look Fat? Aesthetic Labor and Fat Talk as Emotional Labor in a Women's Plus-Size Clothing Store," *Social Problems* 59, no. 4 (November 1, 2012): 481–500; Christine L Williams, *Inside Toyland: Working, Shopping, and Social Inequality* (Berkeley: University of California Press, 2006); Christine L. Williams and Catherine Connell, "'Looking Good and Sounding Right': Aesthetic Labor and Social Inequality in the Retail Industry," *Work and Occupations* 37, no. 3 (2010): 349–377.

36. Traci Parker, *Department Stores and the Black Freedom Movement: Workers, Consumers, and Civil Rights from the 1930s to the 1980s* (Chapel Hill: University of North Carolina Press, 2019).

37. Williams and Connell, "'Looking Good and Sounding Right.'"

38. Yasemin Besen-Cassino, *Consuming Work: Youth Labor in America* (Philadelphia: Temple University Press, 2014).

39. Deborah A. Smith, "Branding Consent: The Role of Employer Brand in Retail Labor Process Control" (PhD dissertation, University of Minnesota, 2011), http://conservancy.umn.edu/handle/11299/101925.

40. Judith Butler, *Precarious Life: The Powers of Mourning and Violence* (Brooklyn, NY: Verso, 2006); David Harvey, *The Condition of Postmodernity: An Enquiry into the Origins of Cultural Change* (Oxford, UK: Blackwell, 1990); Arne L. Kalleberg, "Precarious Work, Insecure Workers: Employment Relations in Transition," *American Sociological Review* 74, no. 1 (2009): 1–22; Kalleberg, *Good Jobs, Bad Jobs*; Guy Standing, *The Precariat: The New Dangerous Class* (London: Bloomsbury, 2016).

41. William H. Whyte, *The Organization Man* (Philadelphia: University of Pennsylvania Press, 2013).

42. Karla Erickson and Jennifer L. Pierce, "Farewell to the Organization Man: The Feminization of Loyalty in High-End and Low-End Service Jobs," *Ethnography* 6, no. 3 (2005): 283–313; Kalleberg, "Precarious Work, Insecure Workers."

43. Stephanie Luce and Naoki Fujita, "Discounted Jobs: How Retailers Sell Workers Short," Retail Action Project, 2012, retailactionproject.org/wp-content/uploads/2012/01/FINAL_RAP.pdf.

44. Stephanie Luce, Sasha Hammad, and Darrah Sipe, "Short Shifted," Retail Action Project, September 2014, http://retailactionproject.org/wp-content/uploads/2014/09/ShortShifted_report_FINAL.pdf.

45. Luce, Hammad, and Sipe, "Short Shifted."

46. Walmart, "Diversity, Equity and Inclusion," 2019, https://corporate.walmart.com/global-responsibility/diversity-equity-and-inclusion.

47. US Census Bureau, "Age & Sex Tables," United States Census Bureau, accessed June 17, 2020, https://www.census.gov/topics/population/age-and-sex/data/tables.html.

48. "The Retail Industry Is Marginalizing Women and People of Color. This Has to Change," Center for Popular Democracy, February 12, 2016, https://populardemocracy.org/news-and-publications/retail-industry-marginalizing-women-and-people-color-has-change.

49. "The Retail Industry Is Marginalizing Women and People of Color."

50. Catherine Ruetschlin and Dedrick Asante-Muhammad, "The Retail Race Divide," Demos, June 2, 2015, https://www.demos.org/research/retail-race-divide-how-retail-industry-perpetuating-racial-inequality-21st-century.

51. H&M, "Inclusion and Diversity," H&M Careers, 2021, https://career.hm.com/content/hmcareer/en_us/workingathm/get-to-know-us/inclusion-and-diversity.html.

52. Luce, Hammad, and Sipe, "Short Shifted."

53. Amber Hollibaugh and Margot Weiss, "Queer Precarity and the Myth of Gay Affluence," *New Labor Forum* 24 (2015): 18–27.

54. Weiss, "Inditex Buys $280M Soho Building for New Zara Store."

55. Samuel R. Delany, *Times Square Red, Times Square Blue* (New York: New York University Press, 1999).

56. Sharon Zukin, *Naked City: The Death and Life of Authentic Urban Places* (Oxford: Oxford University Press, 2010), 127–128.

57. Randy K. Lippert and David Murakami Wood, "The New Urban Surveillance: Technology, Mobility, and Diversity in 21st Century Cities," *Surveillance & Society* 9, no. 3 (2012): 257–262.

58. Michael Corkery, "Walmart Finally Makes It to the Big Apple," *New York Times*, September 16, 2018, https://www.nytimes.com/2018/09/16/business/walmart-jet-nyc.html.

59. Jesse LeCavalier, "All Those Numbers: Logistics, Territory and Walmart," *Places Journal*, May 24, 2010.

Chapter 2

1. John E. G. Bateson et al., "Sifting to Efficiently Select the Right Service Employees," *Organizational Dynamics* 43, no. 4 (2014): 312.

2. Benson, *Counter Cultures*, 25.

3. "May Labour Day: What Is International Workers' Day?," Al Jazeera, 2019, https://www.aljazeera.com/economy/2019/5/1/may-1-labour-day-what-is-international-workers-day.

4. Dora L. Costa, "Hours of Work and the Fair Labor Standards Act: A Study of Retail and Wholesale Trade, 1938–1950," *ILR Review* 53, no. 4 (July 1, 2000): 648–664.

5. Dan Clawson and Naomi Gerstel, *Unequal Time: Gender, Class, and Family in Employment Schedules* (New York: Russell Sage Foundation, 2014); Julia R. Henly and Susan J. Lambert, "Unpredictable Work Timing in Retail Jobs: Implications for Employee Work–Life Conflict," *ILR Review* 67, no. 3 (July 1, 2014): 986–1016; Anna W. Jacobs and Irene Padavic, "Hours, Scheduling and Flexibility for Women in the US Low-Wage Labour Force," *Gender, Work & Organization* 22, no. 1 (January 1, 2015): 67–86; Susan J. Lambert, "Passing the Buck: Labor Flexibility Practices That Transfer Risk onto Hourly Workers," *Human Relations* 61, no. 9 (2008): 1203–1227.

6. Kronos, "Workforce Forecast Manager," accessed January 30, 2017, https://www.kronos.com/resource/download/8236.

7. Esther Kaplan, "The Spy Who Fired Me: The Human Costs of Workplace Monitoring," *Harper's*, March 2015, 34.

8. Kaplan, "The Spy Who Fired Me," 36.

9. Robin Leidner, *Fast Food, Fast Talk: Service Work and the Routinization of Everyday Life* (Berkeley: University of California Press, 1993), 49.

10. Sarah Brayne, "Big Data Surveillance: The Case of Policing," *American Sociological Review* 82, no. 5 (2017): 977–1008.

11. Kronos, "Artificial Intelligence Workforce Management Software," 2020, https://www.kronos.com/products/ai/aimee.

12. Nick Dyer-Witheford, *Cyber-Proletariat: Global Labour in the Digital Vortex* (London: Pluto Press, 2015).

13. Sarah Sharma, *In the Meantime: Temporality and Cultural Politics* (Durham, NC: Duke University Press, 2014).

14. Lambert, "Passing the Buck."

15. Madison Van Oort, "Making the Neoliberal Precariat: Two Faces of Job Searching in Minneapolis," *Ethnography* 16, no. 1 (2015): 74–94.

16. Gillian B. White, "Long Commutes Are Awful, Especially for the Poor," *The Atlantic*, June 10, 2015, https://www.theatlantic.com/business/archive/2015/06/long-commutes-are-awful-especially-for-the-poor/395519/?utm_source=SFTwitter.

17. Javier Auyero, "Patients of the State: An Ethnographic Account of Poor People's Waiting," *Latin American Research Review* 46, no. 1 (2011): 5.

18. Williams and Connell, "'Looking Good and Sounding Right.'"

19. Williams and Connell, "'Looking Good and Sounding Right,'" 361.

20. Aaron Benanav, "Precarity Rising," *Viewpoint Magazine*, June 15, 2015, https://www.viewpointmag.com/2015/06/15/precarity-rising; Hollibaugh and Weiss, "Queer Precarity and the Myth of Gay Affluence."

21. Ashley Mears, "Aesthetic Labor for the Sociologies of Work, Gender, and Beauty," *Sociology Compass* 8, no. 12 (2014): 1330–1343; Lynne Pettinger, "Brand Culture and Branded Workers: Service Work and Aesthetic Labour in Fashion Retail," *Consumption Markets & Culture* 7, no. 2 (2004): 165–184; Williams and Connell, "'Looking Good and Sounding Right.'"

22. Talia Ergas, "H&M Breaks Gender Barriers by Launching a Unisex Denim Line," *Us Weekly*, March 8, 2017, http://www.usmagazine.com/stylish/news/hm-breaks-gender-barriers-by-launching-a-unisex-denim-line-w471028; Eve Peyser, "Zara's Unisex Line Spurs Larger Discussion about Gender," The Cut, March 4, 2016, https://www.thecut.com/2016/03/zaras-ungendered-line-unisex.html.

23. Caitlin Rooney, "Urban Outfitters Latest Retail Outlet to Refuse Trans Customer Access to Fitting Room," ThinkProgress, September 27, 2016, https://thinkprogress.org/urban-outfitters-trans-customer

-aab1ba7f1ca0; Alexi Squire, "Room for Change," *Equal Rights Center* (blog), April 21, 2016, https://equalrightscenter.org/press-releases/room-for-change.

24. Bateson et al., "Sifting to Efficiently Select the Right Service Employees," 312.

25. Eugene Burke and Lesley Kirby, "Dependability and Safety Instrument (DSI) User Guide," SHL Group, 2006.

Chapter 3

1. Portions of this chapter have been adapted from my essay, "Fast Fashion Is Resisting the Retail Apocalypse," published in *Mask Magazine*, 2017.

2. Arlie Russell Hochschild, *The Managed Heart: Commercialization of Human Feeling* (Berkeley: University of California Press, 2003), 146.

3. Julie Beck, "The Concept Creep of 'Emotional Labor,'" *The Atlantic*, November 26, 2018, https://www.theatlantic.com/family/archive/2018/11/arlie-hochschild-housework-isnt-emotional-labor/576637.

4. Joseph Turow, *The Aisles Have Eyes: How Retailers Track Your Shopping, Strip Your Privacy, and Define Your Power* (New Haven, CT: Yale University Press, 2017).

5. Stephanie Baker, "Zara's Recipe for Success: More Data, Fewer Bosses," Bloomberg.com, November 23, 2016, https://www.bloomberg.com/news/articles/2016-11-23/zara-s-recipe-for-success-more-data-fewer-bosses.

6. Bernard Marr, "How Fashion Retailer H&M Is Betting on Artificial Intelligence and Big Data to Regain Profitability," *Forbes*, August 10, 2018, https://www.forbes.com/sites/bernardmarr/2018/08/10/how-fashion-retailer-hm-is-betting-on-artificial-intelligence-and-big-data-to-regain-profitability.

7. Alexandra Ilyashov, "15 Zara Secrets the Press-Shy Brand Hasn't Made Public," Refinery29, March 22, 2016, https://www.refinery29.com/en-us/2016/02/102423/zara-facts.

8. Leah Harper, "Whistleblower Christopher Wylie Joins Fashion Retailer H&M," *The Guardian*, January 31, 2019, http://www.theguardian.com/fashion/2019/jan/31/whistleblower-christopher-wylie-joins-fashion-retailer-h-m; David Styles, "Data and the Dress: What Christopher Wylie Can Teach Fashion," *The Guardian*," August 26, 2019, https://www.theguardian.com/fashion/2019/aug/26/data-and-the-dress-what-christopher-wylie-can-teach-fashion.

9. Karen E. C. Levy, "Digital Surveillance in the Hypermasculine Workplace," *Feminist Media Studies* 16, no. 2 (2016): 361–365.

10. Deborah Cowen, *The Deadly Life of Logistics: Mapping Violence in Global Trade* (Minneapolis: University of Minnesota Press, 2014); Anne Elizabeth Moore, *Threadbare: Clothes, Sex, and Trafficking* (Portland, OR: Microcosm Publishing, 2016); Siddiqi, "Starving for Justice."

11. Ellie Krupnick, "Chemicals in Fast Fashion Revealed in Greenpeace's 'Toxic Threads: The Big Fashion Stitch-Up' (Updated)," *Huffington Post*, November 20, 2012, http://www.huffingtonpost.com/2012/11/20/chemicals-in-fast-fashion-greenpeace-toxic-thread_n_2166189.html.

12. George Ritzer, *The McDonaldization of Society*, 8th ed. (Los Angeles: SAGE Publications, 2014).

13. Marek Korczynski, *Songs of the Factory: Pop Music, Culture, and Resistance* (Ithaca, NY: Cornell University Press, 2014).

14. Spencer Kornhaber, "How Rihanna's 'Work' Works," *The Atlantic*, January 27, 2016, https://www.theatlantic.com/entertainment/archive/2016/01/work-work-work-work-work-rihanna-drake-single-review-anti/431532.

15. Lauren Gail Berlant, *Cruel Optimism* (Durham, NC: Duke University Press, 2011).

16. Benson, *Counter Cultures*; C. Wright Mills, *White Collar: The American Middle Classes* (New York: Oxford University Press, 1951).

17. Jeffrey J. Sallaz, "Permanent Pedagogy: How Post-Fordist Firms Generate Effort but Not Consent," *Work and Occupations* 42, no. 1 (2015): 3–34.

18. Sallaz, "Permanent Pedagogy," 28.

19. Joshua Sperber, "Yelp and Labor Discipline: How the Internet Works for Capitalism," *New Labor Forum* 23 (2014): 68–74.

20. Lynne Pettinger, "On the Materiality of Service Work," *The Sociological Review* 54, no. 1 (2006): 56.

21. Mills, *White Collar*, 177.

22. Simone Browne, *Dark Matters: On the Surveillance of Blackness* (Durham, NC: Duke University Press, 2015), 163.

23. Benson, *Counter Cultures*; Robin D. G. Kelley, "'We Are Not What We Seem': Rethinking Black Working-Class Opposition in the Jim Crow South," *The Journal of American History* 80 (1993): 75–112.

24. Benson, *Counter Cultures*; Crary, *24/7*.

Chapter 4

1. Portions of this chapter have been adapted from my article "The Emotional Labor of Surveillance: Digital Control in Fast Fashion Retail," *Critical Sociology* 45, nos. 7–8 (2019): 1167–1179; and from my chapter "Employing the Carceral Imaginary: An Ethnography of Worker Surveillance in the Retail Industry," in *Captivating Technology: Reimagining Race, Resistance, and Carceral Technoscience*, ed. Ruha Benjamin, 209–223 (Durham, NC: Duke University Press, 2019).

2. National Retail Federation, "National Retail Security Survey," 2020, https://cdn.nrf.com/sites/default/files/2020-07/RS-105905_2020_NationalRetailSecuritySurvey.pdf.

3. Bernard E. Harcourt, *Exposed: Desire and Disobedience in the Digital Age* (Cambridge, MA: Harvard University Press, 2015), 17.

4. danah boyd and Kate Crawford, "Critical Questions for Big Data: Provocations for a Cultural, Technological, and Scholarly Phenomenon," *Information, Communication & Society* 15, no. 5 (2012): 662–679.

5. Ruha Benjamin, *Race after Technology: Abolitionist Tools for the New Jim Code* (Medford, MA: Polity, 2019).

6. Chris Frey, "Revealed: How Facial Recognition Has Invaded Shops—And Your Privacy," *The Guardian*, March 3, 2016, https://www.theguardian.com/cities/2016/mar/03/revealed-facial-recognition-software-infiltrating-cities-saks-toronto.

7. Shoshana Magnet, *When Biometrics Fail: Gender, Race, and the Technology of Identity* (Durham, NC: Duke University Press, 2011); Tom Simonite, "The Best Algorithms Still Struggle to Recognize Black Faces," *Wired*, July 22, 2019, https://www.wired.com/story/best-algorithms-struggle-recognize-black-faces-equally.

8. Joshua Clover, *Riot. Strike. Riot.: The New Era of Uprisings* (Brooklyn, NY: Verso Books, 2016), 125.

9. Kronos, "Data Collection," accessed January 30, 2017, https://www.kronos.com/products/workforce-central-suite/data-collection.

10. Browne, *Dark Matters*; Magnet, *When Biometrics Fail*.

11. Browne, *Dark Matters*; Magnet, *When Biometrics Fail*.

12. Levy, "Digital Surveillance in the Hypermasculine Workplace."

13. David Cooper and Teresa Kroeger, "Employers Steal Billions from Workers' Paychecks Each Year: Survey Data Show Millions of Workers Are Paid Less Than the Minimum Wage, at Significant Cost to Taxpayers and State Economies," Economic Policy Institute, May 10, 2017, https://www.epi.org/publication/employers-steal-billions-from-workers-paychecks-each-year; Amy Traub, "The Steal: The Urgent Need to Combat Wage Theft in Retail," Demos, June 12, 2017, http://www.demos.org/publication/steal-urgent-need-combat-wage-theft-retail.

14. Patrick McGeehan, "New York's Path to $15 Minimum Wage: Uneven, and Bumpy," *New York Times*, April 1, 2016, https://www.nytimes.com/2016/04/02/nyregion/new-yorks-path-to-15-minimum-wage-uneven-and-bumpy.html.

15. Amanda Bronstad, "High Court Orders Apple to Pay Workers for Time Spent Searching Their Bags," The Recorder, 2020, https://www.law.com/therecorder/2020/02/13/high-court-orders-apple-to-pay-workers-for-time-spent-searching-their-bags/; Patrick Kitchin, "CA

Labor Law and Wages for Off-the-Clock Work," *Kitchin Legal* (blog), 2018, https://www.kitchinlegal.com/capturing-wages-for-off-the-clock-work-in-california-retail-stores/; Michael Lore, "$11M Settlement for California Workers' 'Off the Clock' Security Search Pay Claim," Overtime FLSA, May 19, 2020, https://www.overtime-flsa.com/11m-settlement-for-california-workers-off-the-clock-security-search-pay-claim; Overtime Pay Laws, "Nike Retail Workers File Suit to Recover Unpaid OT for Bag Checks," 2019, https://www.overtimepaylaws.org/nike-retail-workers-file-suit-to-recover-unpaid-overtime-for-bag-checks.

16. Bronstad, "High Court Orders Apple to Pay Workers."

17. Becky Yerak, "Mariano's, Kimpton Hotels Sued over Alleged Collection of Biometric Data: 'It's Something Very Personal,'" *Chicago Tribune*, July 21, 2017, http://www.chicagotribune.com/business/ct-employers-biometrics-lawsuits-0723-biz-20170720-story.html.

18. Magnet, *When Biometrics Fail*.

19. Sarah Lazare, "Reckless Security Firm Hired to Protect Dakota Pipeline Company Has Dark Past in Palestine," AlterNet, September 9, 2016, http://www.alternet.org/reckless-security-firm-hired-protect-dakota-pipeline-company-has-dark-past-palestine.

20. Magnet, *When Biometrics Fail*, 50.

21. Ray Hartjen, "LP Made Easy (-ier): POS Exception Reporting with Integrated Video," RetailNext, accessed February 2, 2017, http://retailnext.net/en/blog/lp-made-easy-ier-pos-exception-reporting-with-integrated-video.

22. Lamar Pierce, Daniel C. Snow, and Andrew McAfee, "Cleaning House: The Impact of Information Technology Monitoring on Employee Theft and Productivity," *Management Science* 61, no. 10 (2015): 2299–2319.

23. James Lee, "Forty Years of Researching Retail Loss Prevention," *LP Magazine*, May 15, 2016, 37, http://losspreventionmedia.com/forty-years-of-researching-retail-loss-prevention.

24. Lippert and Wood, "The New Urban Surveillance."

25. Gary T. Marx, "A Tack in the Shoe: Neutralizing and Resisting the New Surveillance," *Journal of Social Issues* 59, no. 2 (2003): 369–390.

26. Benson, *Counter Cultures*, 138.

27. Benson, *Counter Cultures*, 138.

28. Hochschild, *The Managed Heart*; Robin Leidner, "Emotional Labor in Service Work," *The Annals of the American Academy of Political and Social Science* 561, no. 1 (1999): 81–95; Ritzer, *The McDonaldization of Society*.

29. Mears, "Aesthetic Labor for the Sociologies of Work, Gender, and Beauty."

30. Vicky Osterweil, "The Secret Shopper," The New Inquiry, June 4, 2012, http://thenewinquiry.com/essays/the-secret-shopper.

31. Mark Andrejevic, "To Preempt a Thief," *International Journal of Communication* 11 (2017): 879–896; Mark Andrejevic, "Automating Surveillance," *Surveillance & Society* 17, nos. 1–2 (2019): 7–13.

32. Andrejevic, "Automating Surveillance," 11.

33. Brayne, "Big Data Surveillance"; Kate Crawford, "Artificial Intelligence's White Guy Problem," *New York Times*, June 25, 2016, https://www.nytimes.com/2016/06/26/opinion/sunday/artificial-intelligences-white-guy-problem.html?_r=1; Jackie Wang, "'This Is a Story about Nerds and Cops': PredPol and Algorithmic Policing," *E-Flux* (blog), December 2017, http://www.e-flux.com/journal/87/169043/this-is-a-story-about-nerds-and-cops-predpol-and-algorithmic-policing.

34. Virginia Eubanks, *Automating Inequality: How High-Tech Tools Profile, Police, and Punish the Poor* (New York: St. Martin's Press, 2018).

35. National Retail Federation, "National Retail Security Survey," 1.

Chapter 5

1. Portions of this chapter have been adapted from my essay "'Shut It Down!': A Year of Retail Disruptions," *Mask Magazine*, 2015.

2. Salar Mohandesi, "Who Killed Eric Garner?," *Jacobin*, December 12, 2014, http://jacobinmag.com/2014/12/who-killed-eric-garner.

3. Angela Y. Davis, *Are Prisons Obsolete?* (New York: Seven Stories Press, 2011); Ruth Wilson Gilmore, *Golden Gulag: Prisons, Surplus, Crisis, and Opposition in Globalizing California* (Berkeley: University of California Press, 2007).

4. Brayne, "Big Data Surveillance," 995.

5. Miriam Frank, *Out in the Union: A Labor History of Queer America* (Philadelphia: Temple University Press, 2014); Dan Georgakas and Marvin Surkin, *Detroit, I Do Mind Dying* (Boston: South End Press, 1998); Joshua Bloom and Waldo E. Martin, *Black against Empire: The History and Politics of the Black Panther Party* (Berkeley: University of California Press, 2013); Kelley, "'We Are Not What We Seem.'"

6. Benson, *Counter Cultures*, 269.

7. Peter Ikeler, *Hard Sell: Work and Resistance in Retail Chains* (Ithaca, NY: Cornell University Press, 2016).

8. Janice Ruth Fine, *Worker Centers: Organizing Communities at the Edge of the Dream* (Ithaca, NY: Cornell University Press, 2006); Ruth Milkman and Ed Ott, *New Labor in New York: Precarious Workers and the Future of the Labor Movement* (Ithaca, NY: Cornell University Press, 2014).

9. Janice Fine, "Worker Centers: Entering a New Stage of Growth and Development," *New Labor Forum* 20, no. 3 (October 1, 2011): 48.

10. Kate Bronfenbrenner and Dorian T. Warren, "Race, Gender, and the Rebirth of Trade Unionism," *New Labor Forum* 16, nos. 3–4 (2007): 142–148; Kim Moody, *On New Terrain: How Capital Is Reshaping the Battleground of Class War* (Chicago: Haymarket Books, 2017).

11. Jefferson Cowie, *Stayin' Alive: The 1970s and the Last Days of the Working Class* (New York: New Press, 2010), 60; Georgakas and Surkin, *Detroit, I Do Mind Dying*.

12. Cowie, *Stayin' Alive*, 60; Georgakas and Surkin, *Detroit, I Do Mind Dying*.

13. Frank, *Out in the Union*.

14. Hollibaugh and Weiss, "Queer Precarity and the Myth of Gay Affluence."

15. Ikeler, *Hard Sell*, 35.

16. Sonia Singh, "Here's How Zara Retail Workers Won a Union," In These Times, August 31, 2016, http://inthesetimes.com/working/entry/19423/heres_how_zara_retail_workers_won_a_union.

17. Peter Ikeler, "Infusing Craft Identity into a Noncraft Industry," in *New Labor in New York: Precarious Workers and the Future of the Labor Movement* (Ithaca, NY: Cornell University Press, 2014), 116.

18. Rahsaan Mahadeo, "Why Is the Time Always Right for White and Wrong for Us? How Racialized Youth Make Sense of Whiteness and Temporal Inequality," *Sociology of Race and Ethnicity* 5, no. 2 (April 2019): 186–199.

19. Matt Day, "Group of Whole Foods Workers Aims to Unionize," *Seattle Times*, September 6, 2018, https://www.seattletimes.com/business/amazon/group-of-whole-foods-workers-aims-to-unionize-report-says/; Sarah Jones, "A Major Union Election Will Go Ahead at Amazon," Intelligencer, February 5, 2021, https://nymag.com/intelligencer/2021/02/nlrb-oks-vote-to-unionize-amazon-warehouse-in-alabama.html.

20. Alicia Garza, "A Herstory of the #BlackLivesMatter Movement," in *Are All the Women Still White?: Rethinking Race, Expanding Feminisms*, ed. Janell Hobson, 23–28 (Albany: State University of New York Press, 2014).

21. Endnotes, "Brown v. Ferguson," 2015, https://endnotes.org.uk/issues/4/en/endnotes-brown-v-ferguson; Raven Rakia and Aaron Cantu, "The Fight for the Soul of the Black Lives Matter Movement," Gothamist, April 7, 2015, http://gothamist.com/2015/04/07/black_lives_matter_movement.php; Keeanga-Yamahtta Taylor, *From #BlackLivesMatter to Black Liberation* (Chicago: Haymarket Books, 2016).

22. Daniel Politi, "Stop the Parade: NYPD Arrests Ferguson Protesters," *Slate*, November 27, 2014, http://www.slate.com/blogs/the_slatest/2014/11/27/stop_the_parade_nypd_arrests_ferguson_protesters.html.

23. Aamer Madhani, "Arrests across Nation as Protesters Target Black Friday," *USA Today*, November 28, 2014, https://www.usatoday.com/story/news/nation/2014/11/28/crowd-protests-grand-jury-decision-black-friday-st-louis/19624337.

24. Alyssa Figueroa, "8 Developments of the Black Lives Matter Movement Most People Don't Know About," AlterNet, December 15, 2014, https://www.alternet.org/activism/8-developments-black-lives-matter-movement-most-people-dont-know-about.

25. Kim Janssen, "Michigan Avenue Black Friday Protests Cost Stores 25–50 Percent of Sales," *Chicago Tribune*, November 30, 2015, http://www.chicagotribune.com/business/ct-black-friday-mag-mile-fallout-1201-biz-20151130-story.html.

26. Jenna McLaughlin and Sam Brodey, "Eyewitnesses: The Baltimore Riots Didn't Start the Way You Think," *Mother Jones* (blog), April 28, 2015, http://www.motherjones.com/politics/2015/04/how-baltimore-riots-began-mondawmin-purge.

27. Paul Solman, "Why the Freddie Gray Riots Began at a Shopping Mall," *PBS NewsHour*, May 29, 2015, https://www.pbs.org/newshour/economy/answers-baltimores-economic-recovery-start-shopping-mall.

28. Parker, *Department Stores and the Black Freedom Movement.*

29. Mike Davis, "Fortress Los Angeles: The Militarization of Urban Space," in *Variations on a Theme Park: The New American City and the End of Public Space*, ed. Michael Sorkin (New York: Hill and Wang, 1992), 157.

30. Delany, *Times Square Red, Times Square Blue*; Michael Sorkin, *Variations on a Theme Park: The New American City and the End of Public Space* (New York: Macmillan, 1992); Zukin, *Naked City.*

31. Mohandesi, "Who Killed Eric Garner?"

32. Alexandra Klausner, "Zara Stores Accused of Racially Profiling Potential Shoplifters," *Daily Mail*, June 25, 2015, http://www.dailymail.co.uk/news/article-3139350/Fashion-giant-Zara-accused-having-code-word-special-order-profile-black-customers-shoplifters.html.

33. Shaka McGlotten, "Black Data," in *No Tea, No Shade: New Writings in Black Queer Studies* (Durham, NC: Duke University Press, 2016), 270.

34. Simone Browne, "Digital Epidermalization: Race, Identity and Biometrics," *Critical Sociology* 36, no. 1 (2010): 131–150.

35. Benjamin, *Race after Technology*; Cathy O'Neil, *Weapons of Math Destruction: How Big Data Increases Inequality and Threatens Democracy* (New York: Crown, 2016).

36. Jonathan Sterne, "Sounds like the Mall of America: Programmed Music and the Architectonics of Commercial Space," *Ethnomusicology* 41, no. 1 (1997): 27.

37. Aaron Smith, "Abandoned Mall Photos Tell an Eerie American Story," CNNMoney, November 16, 2016, http://money.cnn.com/2016/11/16/news/dead-mall-photos-seph-lawless/index.html.

38. David Francis, "Inside the Anti-Terror Task Force at the Mall of America," *Foreign Policy* (blog), February 23, 2015, https://foreignpolicy.com/2015/02/23/inside-the-anti-terror-task-force-at-the-mall-of-america.

39. Alex Kane, "How Israel Became a Hub for Surveillance Technology," *The Intercept* (blog), October 17, 2016, https://theintercept.com/2016/10/17/how-israel-became-a-hub-for-surveillance-technology; Alice Speri, "Israel Security Forces Are Training American Cops Despite History of Rights Abuses," *The Intercept* (blog), September 15, 2017, https://theintercept.com/2017/09/15/police-israel-cops-training-adl-human-rights-abuses-dc-washington.

40. Daniel Zwerdling, "Under Suspicion at the Mall of America," NPR.org, September 7, 2011, http://www.npr.org/2011/09/07/140234451/under-suspicion-at-the-mall-of-america.

41. Mary Jane Smetanka, "Mall of America Patron Alleges Discrimination," *Star Tribune*, May 6, 2009, http://www.startribune.com/mall-of-america-patron-alleges-discrimination/44505052.

42. Kavita Kumar, "When MOA Shoppers Talk in Cyberspace, the Mall's Likely to Talk Back," *Star Tribune*, 2015, http://www.startri

bune.com/when-you-talk-about-the-mall-of-america-in-cyberspace-these-days-it-s-likely-to-talk-back/352973201.

43. Kumar, "When MOA Shoppers Talk in Cyberspace."

44. Sadie Gurman, "ACLU Wary of Police Using Social Media Tracking Tool," Associated Press, October 6, 2016, www.businessinsider.com/ap-aclu-wary-of-police-using-social-media-tracking-tool-2016-10.

45. Kumar, "When MOA Shoppers Talk in Cyberspace."

46. Geofeedia, "Case Study: Mall of America," http://resources.geofeedia.com/hubfs/Geofeedia_Resources/Geofeedia_UC_MallOfAmerica_Final.pdf.

47. Bill Lindeke, "The Complex Role of Malls: Private but Sort-of-Public Spaces," MinnPost, March 27, 2015, https://www.minnpost.com/cityscape/2015/03/complex-role-malls-private-sort-public-spaces.

48. Cedric J. Robinson, *Black Marxism: The Making of the Black Radical Tradition* (Chapel Hill, NC: University of North Carolina Press, 1983).

49. Associated Press, "Arrests Made as Protest Blocks Roads to Minneapolis Airport," MSNBC, December 23, 2015, http://www.msnbc.com/msnbc/mall-of-america-black-lives-matter-protesters.

50. Lee Fang, "Mall of America Security Catfished Black Lives Matter Activists, Documents Show," *The Intercept* (blog), March 18, 2015, https://theintercept.com/2015/03/18/mall-americas-intelligence-analyst-catfished-black-lives-matter-activists-collect-information.

51. John Reinan and Rochelle Olson, "Charges Dropped against Black Lives Matter over MOA Protest," *Star Tribune*, November 11, 2015, http://www.startribune.com/judge-dismisses-charges-against-black-lives-matter-organizers-of-moa-protest/344894812.

52. Katie Kather, "Black Lives Matter: Activists Seek Dismissal of Charges in Mall of America Protest," *Twin Cities* (blog), July 4, 2015, https://www.twincities.com/2015/07/04/black-lives-matter-activists-seek-dismissal-of-charges-in-mall-of-america-protest.

53. John Fiske, "Shopping for Pleasure: Malls, Power, and Resistance," in *The Consumer Society Reader*, ed. Juliet Schor and Douglas Holt (New York: New Press, 2000).

54. Andrea Smith, "Not Seeing: State Surveillance, Settler Colonialism, and Gender Violence," in *Feminist Surveillance Studies* (Durham, NC: Duke University Press, 2015).

55. Browne, *Dark Matters*; Ruha Benjamin, "Catching Our Breath: Critical Race STS and the Carceral Imagination," *Engaging Science, Technology, and Society* 2 (2016): 145–156.

Conclusion

1. Hochschild, *The Managed Heart*, 203.

2. Hochschild, *The Managed Heart*, 160.

3. MacGillis, *Fulfillment*.

4. Carrie Battan, "M.I.A. Revisits Criticism of */// \Y/*'s 'The Message' in Light of NSA Surveillance Revelations," Pitchfork, June 19, 2013, https://pitchfork.com/news/51229-mia-revisits-criticism-of-ys-the-message-in-light-of-nsa-surveillance-revelations.

5. Kathi Weeks, *The Problem with Work: Feminism, Marxism, Antiwork Politics, and Postwork Imaginaries* (Durham, NC: Duke University Press Books, 2011).

6. Kelley, "'We Are Not What We Seem,'" 75–112.

7. "Mayor de Blasio Announces That NYC Is the Largest City to End Abusive Scheduling Practices," NYC, The Official Website of the City of New York, May 30, 2017, http://www1.nyc.gov/office-of-the-mayor/news/372-17/mayor-de-blasio-speaker-mark-viverito-that-new-york-city-the-largest-city-end.

8. Frey, "Revealed: How Facial Recognition Has Invaded Shops"; Nabil Hassein, "Against Black Inclusion in Facial Recognition," *Decolonized Tech* (blog), August 15, 2017, https://decolonizedtech.com/2017/08/15/against-black-inclusion-in-facial-recognition.

9. Kronos, "Civil Unrest: Police Preparedness, Trends, and Staffing Software Solutions," accessed January 5, 2018, https://www.kronos.com/resources/civil-unrest-police-preparedness-trends-and-staffing-software-solutions.

10. Susan Adams, "Does Goodwill Industries Exploit Disabled Workers?," *Forbes*, July 30, 2013, https://www.forbes.com/sites/susanadams/2013/07/30/does-goodwill-industries-exploit-disabled-workers; Eleanor Goldberg, "These African Countries Don't Want Your Used Clothing Anymore," *Huffington Post*, September 19, 2016, https://www.huffingtonpost.com/entry/these-african-countries-dont-want-your-used-clothing-anymore_us_57cf19bce4b06a74c9f10dd6.

11. Sasha Costanza-Chock, *Design Justice: Community-Led Practices to Build the Worlds We Need* (Cambridge, MA: MIT Press, 2020); Arturo Escobar, *Designs for the Pluriverse: Radical Interdependence, Autonomy, and the Making of Worlds* (Durham, NC: Duke University Press Books, 2018).

12. Benjamin, *Race after Technology*, 197.

13. Our Data Bodies, "Tools," accessed February 21, 2022, https://www.odbproject.org/tools.

Afterword

1. Mónica Marie Zorrilla, "Why George Floyd Protesters in Minneapolis Hit Up Target," *Adweek*, May 29, 2020, https://www.adweek.com/retail/why-demonstrators-protesting-the-death-of-george-floyd-in-minneapolis-keyed-in-on-target.

2. Sarah Bridges, "Retailer Target Branches Out into Police Work," *Washington Post*, January 29, 2006, https://www.washingtonpost.com/archive/politics/2006/01/29/retailer-target-branches-out-into-police-work-span-classbankheadminneapolis-forensics-lab-donations-help-law-enforcement-agenciesspan/32273b10-40fa-4db4-a4a1-88b77eafb891; Bob Giles, "Minneapolis Public-Private Surveillance Effort with Target Corp.," Security Info Watch, April 18, 2012, https://www.securityinfowatch.com/home/article/10702225/minneapolis-publicprivate-surveillance-effort-with-target-corp.

3. International Labor Organization, "ILO Monitor: COVID-19 and the World of Work. 7th Edition," Briefing note, January 25, 2021, http://www.ilo.org/global/topics/coronavirus/impacts-and-responses/WCMS_767028/lang--en/index.htm.

4. Elizabeth Paton, "Myanmar's Defiant Garment Workers Demand That Fashion Pay Attention," *New York Times*, March 12, 2021, https://www.nytimes.com/2021/03/12/business/myanmar-garment-workers-protests.html.

5. Paton, "Myanmar's Defiant Garment Workers Demand That Fashion Pay Attention."

6. Vivian Wang, "Worker Deaths Put Big Tech in China under Scrutiny," *New York Times*, February 1, 2021, https://www.nytimes.com/2021/02/01/business/china-technology-worker-deaths.html.

7. Katitza Rodriguez and Svea Windwehr, "Workplace Surveillance in Times of Corona," Electronic Frontier Foundation, September 10, 2020, https://www.eff.org/deeplinks/2020/09/workplace-surveillance-times-corona.

8. Sebastian Herrera, "Amazon Faces Growing Worker Pressure in Shadow of Alabama Union Vote," *Wall Street Journal*, March 24, 2021, https://www.wsj.com/articles/amazon-faces-growing-worker-pressure-in-shadow-of-alabama-union-vote-11616578202.

9. Tyler Jett, "Could an Amazon Union Form in Iowa? The Teamsters Say They're Organizing Employees," *USA Today*, February 26, 2021, https://www.usatoday.com/story/money/business/2021/02/26/iowa-teamsters-organizing-union-amazon-and-threatening-strike/6841952002.

10. Avi Asher-Schapiro, "Target's Gig Workers Strike over Shipt's New Pay Algorithm," Thompson Reuters Foundation News, October 16, 2020, https://news.trust.org/item/20201016131049-xq8h3.

11. Charmaine Chua, "Organizing against Amazon Requires Strategizing across Global Supply Chains," *Jacobin*, 2021, https://jacobinmag.com/2021/04/amazon-global-supply-chains-organizing-unionize-logistics.

Appendix

1. Leslie Salzinger, *Genders in Production: Making Workers in Mexico's Global Factories* (Berkeley: University of California Press, 2003).

2. Mingwei Huang, "Vulnerable Observers: Notes on Fieldwork and Rape," *The Chronicle of Higher Education*, October 12, 2016, https://www.chronicle.com/article/vulnerable-observers-notes-on-fieldwork-and-rape.

3. Kevin Van Meter, *Guerrillas of Desire: Notes on Everyday Resistance and Organizing to Make a Revolution Possible* (Chico, CA: AK Press, 2017).

4. Christina Sharpe, "Black Life, Annotated," *The New Inquiry* (blog), August 8, 2014, https://thenewinquiry.com/black-life-annotated.

5. David Harvey, *Rebel Cities: From the Right to the City to the Urban Revolution* (Brooklyn, NY: Verso Books, 2012).

6. Asad Haider and Salar Mohandesi, "Workers' Inquiry: A Genealogy," *Viewpoint Magazine*, September 27, 2013, https://www.viewpointmag.com/2013/09/27/workers-inquiry-a-genealogy; Jamie Woodcock, "The Workers' Inquiry from Trotskyism to Operaismo: A Political Methodology for Investigating the Workplace," *Ephemera: Theory & Politics in Organization* 14, no. 3 (2014): 493–451.

7. Madison Van Oort, "Employing the Carceral Imaginary: An Ethnography of Retail Worker Surveillance," in *Captivating Technology: Reimagining Race, Resistance, and Technoscience*, ed. Ruha Benjamin (Durham, NC: Duke University Press, 2019).

8. Chelsea Barbaras, Colin Doyle, J. B. Rubinovitz, and Karthik Dinakar, "Studying Up: Reorienting the Study of Algorithmic Fairness Around Issues of Power," *ACM Conference on Fairness, Accountability, and Transparency, Barcelona, Spain, January 27–30, 2020*. New York: ACM, 2017.

Index

Note: Page numbers in *italics* indicate figures and page numbers in **bold** indicate tables.